Variegreat!

New Dimensions in Traditional Quilts

by Linda Glantz

Located in Paducah, Kentucky, the American Quilter's Society (AQS), is dedicated to promoting the accomplishments of today's quilters. Through its publications and events, AQS strives to honor today's quiltmakers and their work — and inspire future creativity and innovation in quiltmaking.

EDITOR: JANE R. MCCAULEY

TECHNICAL EDITOR: HELEN SQUIRE

BOOK DESIGN/ILLUSTRATIONS: ANGELA SCHADE

COVER DESIGN: TERRY WILLIAMS

PHOTOGRAPHY: CHARLES R. LYNCH

Library of Congress Cataloging-in-Publication Data

Glantz, Linda

    Variegreat! new dimensions in traditional quilts / by Linda Glantz

                p.   cm.

    ISBN 0-89145-795-X

    1. Variegation--Patterns.

quilts--United States--History.   I. Title.

TT835.C3735   1997

746.46'041--dc21   97-25847

                                     CIP

Additional copies of this book may be ordered from: American Quilter's Society, PO Box 3290, Paducah, KY 42002-3290 @ $19.95. Add $2.00 for postage & handling.

Printed in the U.S.A. by Image Graphics, Paducah, KY

Dedication

I would like to dedicate *Variegreat!* to some very important people in my life.

First, my husband Eric, for all his positive support through this entire project;

My good friend, Sue Bryant, for being there every minute;

My son, Patrick, for helping to name the quilt projects in this book; and my daughter Rachael, and to my parents for raising me to believe in myself.

To Pat Young, Jean Gauthier, Joan Smith, Lynn Sweeney, Barb Rouse, Janet Root, Ellen Reed, and Donna Whipple, all friends and members of Country Neighbors Quilt Guild, Chapter 2, without whom this book would not have been possible.

To the "International Sister Guild Partnership Program" founded in 1994 by the Country Neighbors Quilt Guild. Several project quilts in this book are named for great friends I have made through this program, and the CIRCLE OF FRIENDS quilt is in honor of all countries involved. For more information, write to them, c/o Apple Country Quilt Shop, 4719 Bennetts Corners Road, Holley, New York 14470.

Preface

Just as the proverbial "light bulb going off in the head" goes, is how this project began for me. On the way back from a quilting workshop, two of my teachers and I were discussing ways to promote a program in the shop and the guild. The more I thought about the idea of promoting this specific project, the more it made a lot of sense to me.

As a quilt shop owner and founder and coordinator of Country Neighbors Quilt Guild, I work each day with both novice and experienced quilters who are looking for designs that are easy and really work. Variegreat! is simple and very successful, and it can be applied to both traditional and contemporary quilt blocks, both pieced and appliquéd.

Traditionally, variegated meant working with solid color fabrics — but not anymore! All the tone-on-tone prints available today to quilters provide great texture and a step up from solid color gradations. In this book, you will find a very straightforward way to apply Variegreat! to many quilt blocks. Whether a quilt is made from a single pattern or different ones, you will see spectacular results. There's also advice about choosing fabrics for the program and how to make them work for you. Be prepared to look at traditional and appliquéd blocks in a brand new way!

Linda Glantz

Contents

Introduction

Variegreat!

The definition of variegation is "to diversify in external appearance, especially with colors." As I developed designs for this book, I found many different ways to give traditional quilt blocks real flair simply by breaking the blocks into their different components and rearranging them, also using gradations of color to change their visual appeal.

The Variegreat! program will alter colors within the same color families, for example, light, medium, and dark shades of blue; light, medium, and dark shades of green; light, medium, and dark shades of purple, etc. This does not necessarily mean that you may use only three shades. The amount of contrast or subtleness of the variegation is your decision. Once a block is broken down, you choose what is appropriate for your design.

To better understand the program and to begin enjoying the techniques we discuss, you will need to know a few working terms.

Segments: Once you have chosen your variegated colors and design, you will cut your fabrics into strips and sew them together. These strips are called segments.

Groupings: After the segments are sewn together and the block pieces have been cut with a template or ruler, this will be called a grouping.

Color shade: This is a unit of color within a segment. The number of colors will range from three to eight or more.

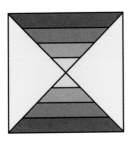

1 Choosing a Block

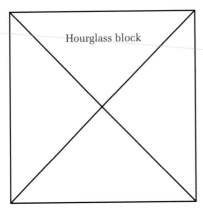

Hourglass block

Illustration 1-1
Hourglass block

The simplest way to learn to use this design program is to start with a basic block. As an example, I have chosen a simple Hourglass block (Illus. 1-1). I selected this block because it is easy to work with and provides great design components.

Begin by drawing some horizontal lines through two of the triangles to activate them into the Variegreat! design program (Illus. 1-2).

Using a pencil to do some shading, you can now variegate these two segments and get an idea of how this changes the original block into something wonderful (Illus. 1-3).

See what happens when you put several of these blocks together (Illus. 1-4)? Before you know it, you have designed a beautiful quilt with great impact!

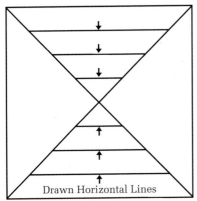

Drawn Horizontal Lines

Illustration 1-2

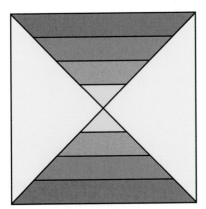

Illustration 1-3
Shaded dark to light

Illustration 1-4
Variegated design using nine blocks

Now try the Ohio Star block which has more variables. Draw segment lines (Illus. 1-5) and then shade (Illus. 1-6). This block provides many options. Why not see how many you can create? It is especially easy to incorporate Variegreat! with blocks that use squares and triangles, although diamonds, curved patches, and appliqué blocks can also be adapted with a little skill and practice.

For practice, draw a block outline on the grid on the next page. Then, place lines through different segments of the block and use your pencil or colored pencils to shade them. This will give you an idea of how easy it is to work with this program (Illus. 1-7).

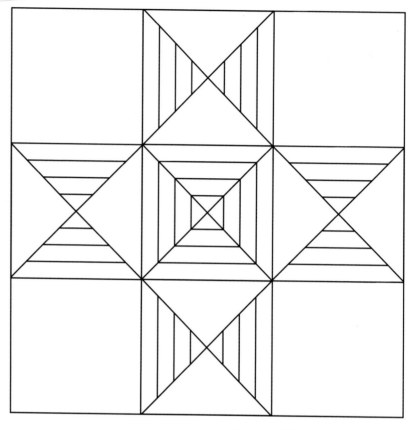

Above — Illustration 1-5
Ohio Star block with segment lines

Left — Illustration 1-6
Ohio Star block with shaded
variegated segments

Illustration 1-7
Use this grid with a block of your choice and see what options you create.

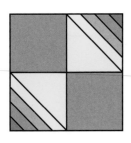

2 Color Shading

To get a good idea of how your block is going to take shape and ultimately what design you will want to use to reach your final goal — a beautiful quilt, you will need to experiment with color shading.

One way is to draw your block, or blocks if you are using more than one, on graph paper and shade different areas to help you decide your design. If you own a computer and a quilt design program for your computer, this process is made easier. You can use the draw program in your computer to outline your block and to draw your segment lines, and use the color system to shade the segments into groupings. Set up your quilt design program to get a good idea of block placements and the different effects you will get by moving them around.

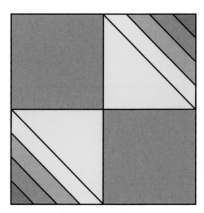

Illustration 2-1
Variegreat! block

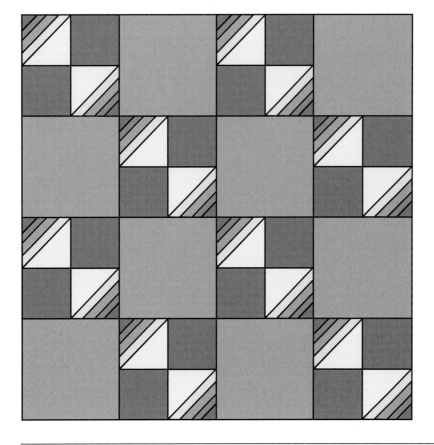

There are several ways to work with these blocks to broaden the use of the Variegreat! program. For example, look at the block in Illus. 2-1 above. You can repeat or alternate the blocks with plain ones (Illus. 2-2) or use the same block throughout the quilt to get a unique design (Illus. 2-3).

Illustration 2-2
Variegreat! block with alternating plain blocks

Notice that when the groupings in one block butt against another block, you get a continuation of the variegation. As you change shadings, you will discover a new aspect of design emerges. Patterns show up in the quilt design that would never have existed without this program.

You may want to get really creative and alternate your block with a plain block, alternate your block with a second new Variegreat! design, or add another block that is not variegated. For example, let's use the same block and alternate it with a plain block (Illus. 2-4).

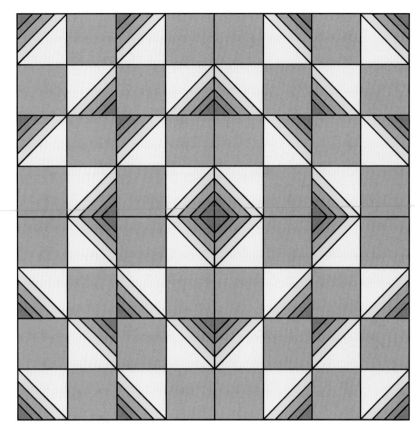

Illustration 2-3
Variegreat! design using the same block throughout the quilt

Illustration 2-4
Variegreat! block alternated with a plain block

Choose a second non-variegated nine-patch block to set the quilt in motion (Illus. 2-5).

In Illus. 2-6, notice how mixing the blocks creates another beautiful design. Don't be inhibited by this process. It is fun and exciting to design, and you will find that you will look at traditional as well as innovative quilt blocks in a whole new way!

Illustration 2-5
Variegreat! block alternated with a non-variegated Nine-Patch block

Illustration 2-6
Variegreat! and Nine-Patch blocks rearranged to create another unique design

Determining the size of the block

Now that I have your interest, you are probably full of ideas and have begun looking at different blocks for experimenting. Most block patterns you choose need to be altered to fit the dimensions of your quilt.

Be flexible in this area and go with a size that works for the block, adjusting the exact measurement for the whole quilt.

First, decide in what category your block falls; for example, is it a Four-Patch, a Five-Patch, a Nine-Patch, etc.? Next, determine into what increments the block is divided. If it is a Four-Patch, there should be four equal divisions across and down the block. If it is a Five-Patch, then there are five equal divisions.

In most cases, you can determine size by the measurement of each divisional block. For instance, if the individual block is 1" in a Nine-Patch division, then the block size will be 3". If the block is 1½" in a Five-Patch division, then the block size will be 7½". If the block is 2" in a Four-Patch division (of a Sixteen-Patch block), then the blocks will be 8", etc.

Tables to Determine Block Size

Basic Nine-patch	Basic Five-patch	Basic Four-patch	Basic Four-patch divided in half
1" equals 3" block	1" equals 5" block	2" equals 4" block	2" equals 8" block
2" equals 6" block	2" equals 10" block	3" equals 6" block	3" equals 12" block
3" equals 9" block	3" equals 15" block	4" equals 8" block	4" equals 16" block
4" equals 12" block	4" equals 20" block	5" equals 10" block	5" equals 20" block
5" equals 15" block		6" equals 12" block	
6" equals 18" block		7" equals 14" block	
		8" equals 16" block	
		9" equals 18" block	

Once you have decided to variegate a quilt block and have broken it down into its components, you need to decide how many segments you would like. There is no specific rule to apply here, except not to make too many divisions. Sometimes too many variegations become less discernible in your design and can run into each other. Of course, the other problem with too many variegations is finding enough fabric matches.

In a color progression, more gradation colors will give a softer effect to the quilt. Look at the quilt, "Beauty and the Beast" (p. 88) in the project section. This quilt has seven gradation colors which give a quieter look to the background. The bright orange in the piecing adds zip to the overall appearance. The "Desert Star" quilt (p. 57) has five gradation colors and also has a subtle overall appearance.

Sometimes, keeping things simple produces the best general appearance. Using only three gradation colors, a light, medium, and dark, is plenty for a quilt. Solid color gradations work very well, but try also to work with fabrics that have some texture to make the quilt more interesting.

I have found that working with anywhere from a minimum of three gradation colors to a maximum of eight works best. One exception is to enlarge a quilt block to 18" or 24" which gives more area in the pieced block to break down.

Breaking down the quilt block

Now that you have decided what part of your quilt block you want to variegate, you need to make a template of that block segment. You can make one out of plastic; you will need to be able to draw on the template. Measure the template. If you have a square template that measures 4½" by 4½", you can easily break this down into four variegated segments. Divide the block measurement by 4 and you will have 1" segments with seam allowances on each end. Draw these four 1" increments onto your template. These lines will be especially helpful when you need to line up your seams for accurate cutting (Illus. 3-1).

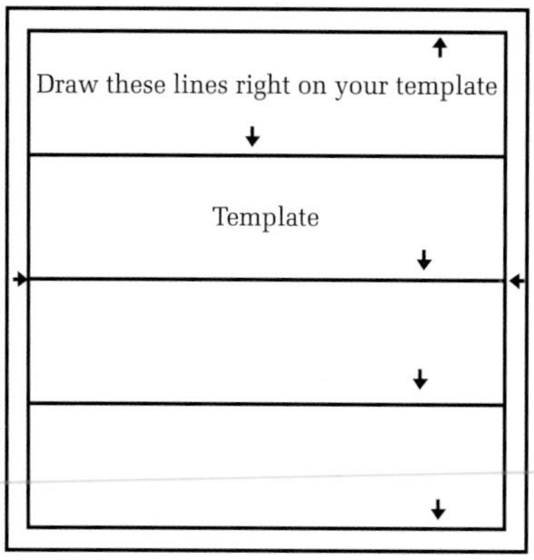

You now know you need 1" segments, but you still have to add the seam allowance to both sides. If your measurement is 1", you will be cutting a 1½" segment strip. Since you have broken the block down into four equal segments, you will be cutting a 1½" strip for each of the four variegated colors you will be using.

You may choose to break your segments into uneven strips. For example, you might want your lightest color to be wider than your medium or dark color. In that case, you may break it down to any measurement, but be sure to add seam allowances to each side, or your grouping strip will not be wide enough for your template (Illus. 3-2).

Assembling Variegreat! segments into groupings

After you've measured and determined a size plus seam allowance for your variegated strips, sew those strips together, lengthwise. I find it easiest to begin with the darkest color and sew to the lightest color. If you are using blue gradations, for instance, start with the darkest blue, then the medium blue, and then the lightest blue (Illus. 3-3).

Always press your seams open when making your groupings. A note about pressing — make a line on your ironing board that runs the length of it either with masking tape or a permanent marker that will not bleed onto the fabric. You can purchase ironing board covers that have ruler markings on them. It is important to have a guide for pressing groupings as they will tend to warp without a straight edge to follow.

Once you have pressed your grouping, it is time to cut your pieces from that strip. Lay your strip out lengthwise on a cutting mat in front of you. Place your template on top of the strip and cut out your piece. We call this your grouping piece because it now contains your Variegreat! grouping. Continue to cut along the strip with your rotary cutter, matching up the seam lines on your template with the seams on the grouping strip. This will help you make accurate cuts. You may also use angle rulers to do this cutting. If you choose to do this,

Illustration 3-1
Using template plastic, draw lines directly onto template.

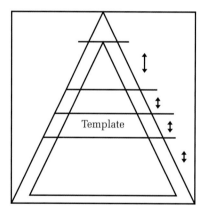

Illustration 3-2
Measure distance.
Add ¼" to each side.

Illustration 3-3
Grouping sewn dark to light.
Press seams open.

place ¼" masking tape on the ruler to mark your seam guides and help you cut accurately (Illus.3-4).

Assemble your cut pieces into your block. There is one small catch. Depending on where you have chosen to variegate your block, you may find that some altered seams butt against other ones in the same block or at the point where you sew one completed block to another. Make sure you pin these seams together before sewing so they match accurately. Do not try the push and pull method under your presser foot; it rarely works. Many of these pieces are cut on the bias and will distort.

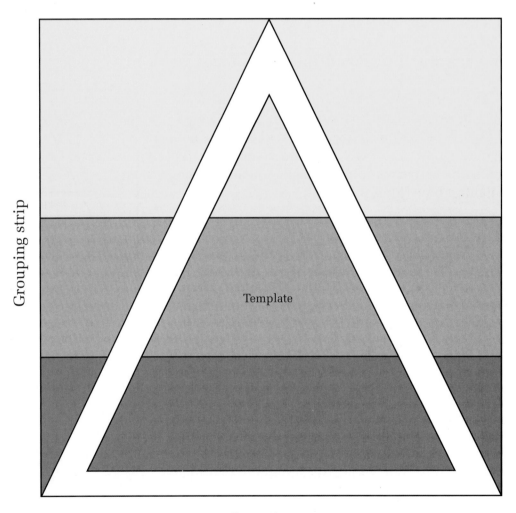

Illustration 3-4
Lay template on grouping strip.

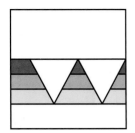

4 Selecting & Arranging Fabric

After you have decided on your design, you need to select appropriate fabrics to make that design come alive. Traditionally, gradations have been selected in solid colors largely because fabrics that were not solids were multicolored prints. When you walk into a fabric shop, you find many alternatives to solids, such as tone-on-tone fabrics, single, and two-color ones. You certainly have a larger selection in most quilt stores which gives you many more options.

In this book, I have worked mostly with tone-on-tone, single, and two color fabrics. However, in the appliqué pattern "Floral Fantasy," on page 122, I used hand-dyed solid colors. The choice is up to you; however, I do encourage you to stretch tradition a little and try some of the newer fabrics. After you have collected your stash, there are a couple of ways you can arrange them from dark to light (Illus. 4-1) and placed outward from the darkest (Illus. 4-2).

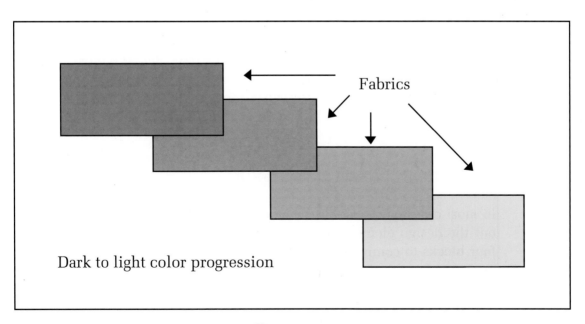

Fabrics

Dark to light color progression

Illustration 4-1
Fabrics arranged from dark to light.

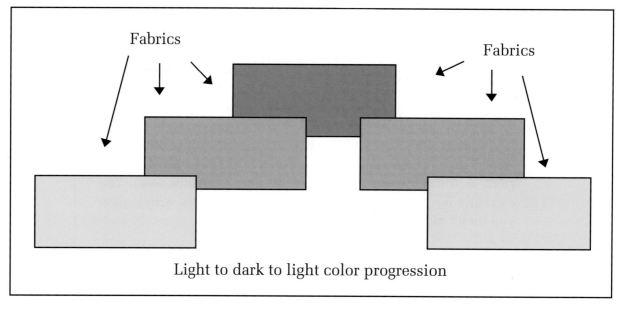

Fabrics

Fabrics

Light to dark to light color progression

Illustration 4-2
Fabric tones arranged outward from the center.

Once you get an idea of your progression, you will want to choose a background fabric that compliments the gradation, not one that takes away from it. Many fabric stores now carry mottled, "cracked-ice," or marbled fabrics, etc. Backgrounds textured to resemble the sky work well, too. Use your imagination. I like background fabrics with movement so that when you cut them apart, each piece looks a little different.

Determining the size of your quilt

In most cases, you need a particular number of blocks to bring out the design element in your quilt. Some designs take only four blocks to complete, others can take as many as 36 blocks. To determine the size of your quilt, you need to figure out how many blocks it will take to complete your design layout, then size your blocks accordingly. (See Chapter 3, page 13 on how to enlarge or reduce your block size.)

Computing fabric requirements

In order to determine how much fabric you need to construct your variegated block components, decide the following:

    a) how many variegation segments you will be using

    b) how wide the strips are in each segment

    c) how many cuts you can get from each grouping strip.

For example, if you are using the 4½" square segment that was described in the previous chapter and you are subdividing it into four variegated segments, your strips will be 1½" wide for each color. Once you sew these strips together lengthwise, working with a 44" wide fabric you can get roughly nine 4½" group cuts from that set of strips. If you are working with smaller fabric pieces such as fat quarters, then you will be cutting 22" lengths. You will get four grouping cuts from that set of strips. You can get your number by dividing 4½" into 44" (or 22" for fat quarters).

If it is going to take twenty 4½" groupings to make your quilt, and if you are using a 44" wide fabric, you will get nine cuts out of that width. It will take four grouping strips to get twenty 4½" cuts. Multiply 1½" (the width of your individual color strip) x four to get 6" by 44" of fabric. Now we know that you will need ¼ yard of 44" wide fabric for each color in your Variegreat! grouping. However, I would buy ¼ yard extra to allow for shrinkage before cutting strips. It is always best to buy a little more in case of a cutting error.

If you are working with fat quarters, which are so popular, you can cut four groupings from each strip. You need 20 cuts, so you will need five strip groupings in order to get the number you need. Five x 1½" = a 7½" x 22" piece. A fat quarter will be sufficient to accommodate the 20 cuts.

When working with square grouping cuts, you waste very little fabric. However, working with triangles or other odd-shaped cuts does waste some fabric. Look at the "Mint Julep" project on page 36 for an example of a quilt that will use the extra cuts left over from your grouping cuts.

When you are cutting a triangle template from a grouping strip and you only need the base of the triangle cut on the dark gradation, inverse triangles will be left over after you have made your quilt blocks (Illus. 4-3). There are many things you can do with them. For example, extra pieces can be used to create an interesting border, such as the quilt on page 51, named "Estelle." Use your imagination and incorporate your leftovers into another block or a new quilt design.

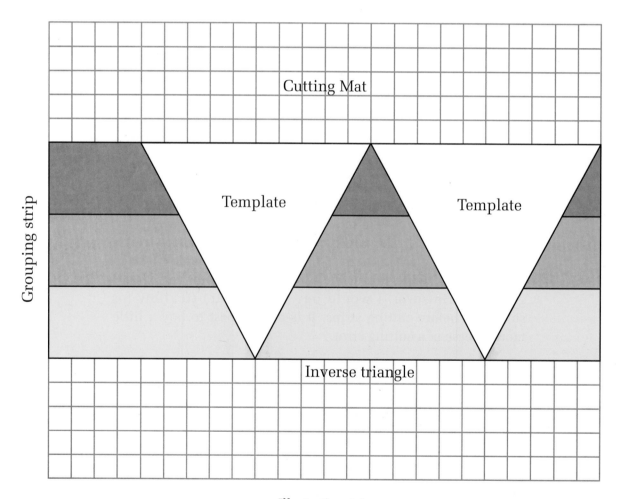

Illustration 4-3

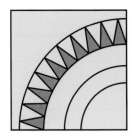

5 Block Construction Methods

Throughout the patterns and designs you create, there are some basic construction methods you will find very helpful if you take the time to learn them. They help save cutting time as well as time spent repairing mismatched seams. There are three such methods in this chapter — squaring blocks, magic triangles, and half-square triangles.

Squaring blocks

This term applies to a completed block as well as its components. As the parts of a block are finished, I find that taking the time to trim an oversized piece is helpful in the long run. You will need a square ruler to do this. In Illus. 5-1, a square ruler with a diagonal line has been placed on top of a block component. If you place the diagonal line of the ruler on the template's seam line and use the ruler measurements, you can trim away excess fabric on the top and the side with your rotary cutter. Simply turn the block and complete trimming on the other sides.

This technique will prove invaluable when trying to match seams and also when working with bias edges.

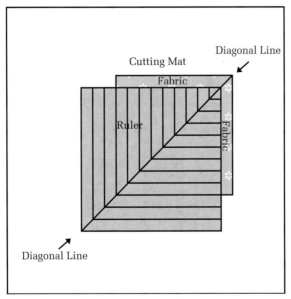

Illustration 5-1
Squaring a block matching diagonal seam with
diagonal line on ruler

Magic triangles

I borrowed this term from my dear quilting friend, Sue. Magic triangles is basically a quick way to use two triangles to form a square. This is achieved through the construction of a grid directly on fabric.

Cut the two fabric pieces to the appropriate size for your pattern. Place these two pieces right sides together and lay them flat on your cutting table. With a fabric marker or pencil, draw the grid directly onto the top piece. Once the grid is drawn, you may add ¼" seam allowances to either side of the diagonal grid lines, or you may sew with a ¼" foot on either side (Illus. 5-2a).

Next, cut apart your blocks on the straight lines of the grid first, then cut apart on the diagonal. Always cut down the center of the diagonal stitching (Illus. 5-2b).

Open the blocks and press seams toward the darker side. When this step is completed, square your new block components.

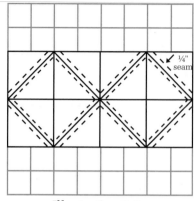

Illustration 5-2a
Placing fabrics right sides together, draw grid lines onto fabric. Begin sewing on the quarter inch mark

Half-square triangles

This type of triangle is simply half of a square cut on the diagonal, yielding two triangles. This technique (Illus. 5-3) is used to save cutting time. Dimensions for the square are given in the pattern. However, if you would like to use this method to cut triangles for your own designs, you will need to figure the size of the square you need to cut. Determine what the finished length of the short side of the triangle needs to be, then add ⅞" to this number. Cut the square to this size, then cut the square apart on the diagonal.

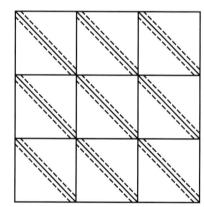

Illustration 5-2b
Fabric right sides together with grid lines and sewn lines.

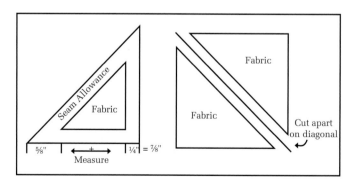

Illustration 5-3
Determine size of triangle by measuring finished size of short side, then add ⅞" to that measurement. Cut a square that measurement, then cut square in half on the diagonal.

Quarter-square triangles

This method of cutting produces two bias cut edges on the triangles so it is not recommended as often in these projects. The variegated triangle groupings also have bias edges, and when they have to butt against each other, accurate piecing is difficult. However, since not all blocks are constructed the Variegreat! way, you may find this method useful.

To make a quarter-square triangle, you need to cut a square apart on the diagonal twice to yield four quarter-square triangles. To determine what size square will give the correct size triangles, measure the long side of the triangle, and add 1¼" to that figure. Cut the square apart twice on the diagonal (Illus. 5-4).

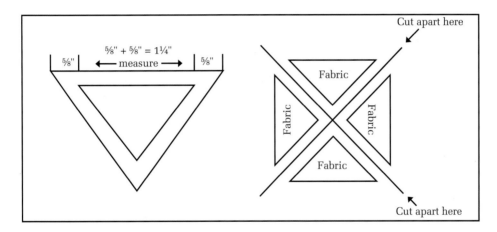

Illustration 5-4

Paper piecing — Log Cabin blocks

There is a paper piecing pattern included in the section for the New York Nights quilt, shown on page 85. You may make copies of this block on a copy machine for the number of blocks you will need for your quilt.

Sewing hint: Try setting your sewing machine on a tighter stitch than usual when sewing through paper and fabric. It will make tearing away the paper easier after the block is completed.

As shown in Illustration 5-5, place your center square of fabric on the unmarked side of the paper, right side showing, directly over the center square. If you hold this up to a light or window, you can see through the paper to tell if you have lined up your fabric correctly.

Place your next strip of fabric so it extends over the second line and on either side of the center square. Put the right sides together with the first square of fabric. You can pin these to the paper on the marked side so that you may slide the paper and fabric neatly under your presser foot. Now, sew on this line (Illus. 5-6). Remove the fabric and paper from under your presser foot and press the second piece over that area on your paper or away from the center piece. Trim away excess seam allowance.

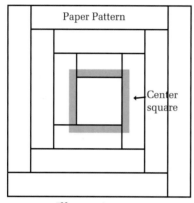

Illustration 5-5

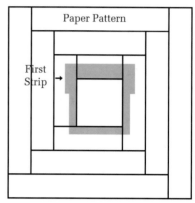

Illustration 5-6

Place fabric under paper pattern directly over center square, wrong side of fabric on paper. Then, place second fabric over first fabric (right sides together) over line 2 and on either side of center square. Sew on line 2.

Take the fabric for third piece and place on unmarked side of paper once again, right sides together, with center square. Sew on third line. Press.

Continue with this method until you have sewed on all the lines and completed your log cabin square. Use your square ruler to trim accurately. Then, carefully tear away the paper. If it is difficult to tear, try soaking the block in water for a minute.

Paper piecing — New York Beauty blocks

Cut out the paper foundation for piecing ¼" around the bold line for the pointed arcs. This is the section to be paper pieced. Make two piles of strips, one dark and one light. You will start with the dark strip at the end on the left. Again, holding the paper up to light or a window, line up the strip, face up, at the end of the paper foundation with the seam allowance extending over the line (Illus. 5-7a). Sew on the first stitching line (solid line). Press fabric. Trim excess seam allowance. Now place dark fabric (right sides together) along the next line, extending past sewing line. (To check, hold up to light to make sure you have extended fabric over the sewing line.) Sew on this line, and press fabric away once again. Trim away excess seam allowance. Continue in this manner, first dark, then light, then dark, etc., until you have completed the paper foundation (Illus. 5-7b). Peel away paper carefully from fabric when all sewing has been completed.

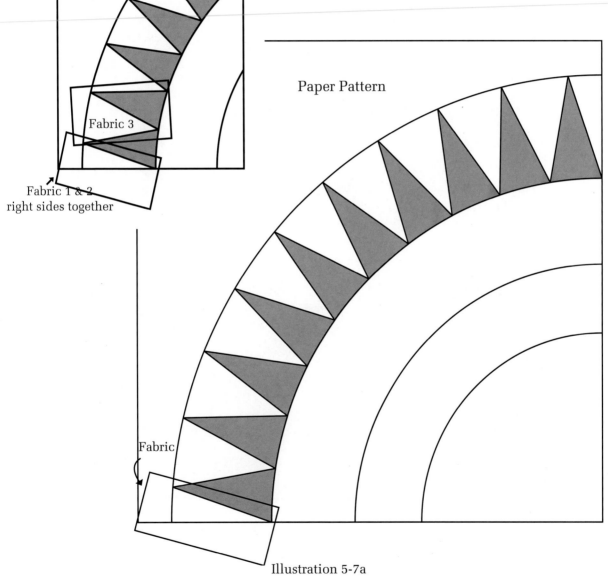

Illustration 5-7a
Start with dark strip at end on left. Line up the strip with seam allowance extending over the line. Sew on line with fabric underneath the paper.

Illustration 5-7b (detail)
Line up second piece on first stitching line. Sew on line. Press fabric away from first fabric. Trim seam allowance. Add third piece in the same way.

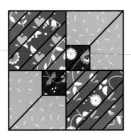

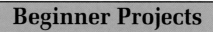

Town Square

TOWN SQUARE, 38" x 38"
Designed by Linda Glantz
Quilted by Pat Young

Mint Julep

MINT JULEP, 38" x 38"
Designed by Linda Glantz
Quilted by Sue Bryant

Materials:

⅓ yd. dark green

⅓ yd. medium green

⅓ yd. medium light green

1½ yds. background fabric

½ yd. medium pink for Nine-Patch

½ yd. border (double for second wallhanging)

1½ yds. backing plus rod pocket (double for second wallhanging)

1¼ yds 45" low loft batting (double for second wallhanging)

⅓ yd. binding cross-grain binding (double for second wallhanging)

Cut:

(5) 1½" x 42" for each green shade

(5½) 2½" x 42" medium pink

(4) 2½" x 42" background fabric

(3) 7¼" strips. Re-cut into 7¼" squares. Quick cut squares into quarter-square triangles, as explained on in Chapter 5, page 23. This should give you 20 triangles. For hand cutting, template #1 is provided on page 103.

(4) 4½" x 42" strips for border. The extra length allows for mitered corners.

For variegated groupings, sew three strips together lengthwise. Sew from light to dark, pressing seams open. Lay two grouping strips, right sides together, one with dark strip on top, another with dark strip on the bottom, so that seams match and you have a smooth surface for cutting. Place Variegreat! triangle template

#1 on top of strip at one end. Make approximately 5 to 6 consecutive cuts per grouping strip. Do the same with the remainder of the strips. Separate triangles, dark bottoms in one pile, light ones in second pile. Place variegated grouping and background triangles together as shown (Illus.1).

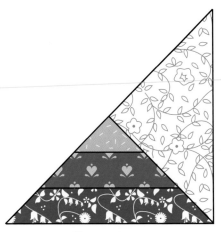

Illustration 1

Now, sew halves together with light-based pieces to create an hourglass (Illus. 2a). Then, sew dark ones together (Illus. 2b). Press seams toward background fabric. Square up to 6½" using 3¼" lines on ruler.

Illustration 2a
Assembly diagram for light-based blocks

Illustration 2b
Assembly diagram for dark-based blocks

For Nine-Patch, using 2½" x 42" strips of background fabric and pink fabric, sew a dark, light, and dark strip together. Press seams to the darker side. Re-cut again into 2½" segments. You will need (9) segments (Illus. 3). Square template #2 is provided on page 103 for traditional methods.

Sew light, dark, and light strips together. Press towards the dark. Cut again into 2½" segments. You will need (18) segments (Illus. 4).

Illustration 3

Illustration 4

Place segments together as shown. Sew and press center seams away from center. Make (9) Nine-Patch blocks (Illus. 5).

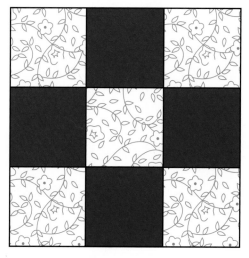

Illustration 5
Sew segments together.

Arrange the two Variegreat! hourglass blocks and the Nine-Patch blocks in the pattern indicated on the quilt diagram (Illus. 6). Assemble outer border. (Refer to quilt photograph on page 31.)

Quilt and bind as desired.

Illustration 6
Quilt block placement for MINT JULEP

With any extra Variegreat! pieces, you can use this idea for another quilt (Illus. 7).

Illustration 7
Look what you can do with those extra pieces!

Monkeying Around

MONKEYING AROUND, 36" x 36"
Designed by Linda Glantz
Quilted by Lynn Sweeney

Materials:

For this project, I recommend ¼ yd. cuts instead of fat quarters for ease in cutting, although they can be used if available.

¼ yd. each of dark red, medium dark red, medium light red, light red

¼ yd. each of dark gray, medium dark gray, medium light gray, light gray

⅝ yd. background

⅛ yd. first border

Scraps for second border

¼ yd. binding

1¼ yd. 45" batting

1¼ yd. 45" backing

Cut:

From background fabric, cut strip 7⅞" wide. Re-cut strip into 7⅞" squares. Cross-cut squares into quarter-square triangles or use template #1. You will need to cut (32) triangles.

For Four-Patch center:

Cut (1) strip of background 1⅞" x 42" and (1) strip of dark red, 1⅞" x 42". Sew these strips together lengthwise and press toward dark fabric.

Cut (1) strip of light gray, 1⅞" x 42" and (1) strip of background, 1⅞" by 42". Sew these strips together lengthwise. Press toward dark fabric.

Lay these strips out lengthwise and with a straight-edge ruler, re-cut them apart every 1⅞". Or you can cut individual squares using template #2. You will need to cut (16) of each color set. Sew one red set to one gray set to create your Four-Patch (Illus. 1).

Illustration 1
Assembly diagram for Four-Patch block

Cut (2) strips of background fabric, 3" x 42." Re-cut these into (16) 3" squares. Re-cut again on diagonal into half-square (32) triangles. Or, you may use template #3 to cut these triangles.

Cut (2) strips 3" x 42" each of medium light red and medium light gray. Cut into (16) 3" squares. Cut again on the diagonal for half-square triangles; you will need 16 of each color. You may also cut any of these triangles using template #3. Sew these triangles to your Four-Patch, adding one gray triangle to one side and one red to the opposite side. Then, add two background triangles to the other side, pressing seams to the outside (Illus. 2).

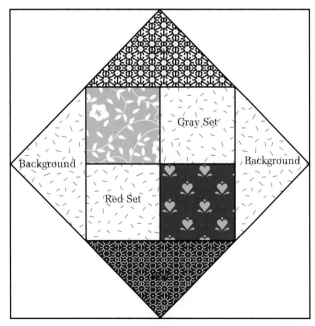

Illustration 2

Cut (2) strips 4" x 42" of background fabric. Cut into (16) 4" squares and re-cut on diagonal to make (32) half-square triangles. You may use template #4 to cut these triangles.

Cut two strips 4" x 42" each of medium dark red and medium dark gray. Cut into (16) 4" squares and re-cut on diagonal once into 16 half-square triangles of each color. You may cut any of these triangles using template #4. Build up the block by adding two background triangles on opposite sides, pressing seams to outside, then sewing one gray and one red triangle to the other sides (Illus. 3).

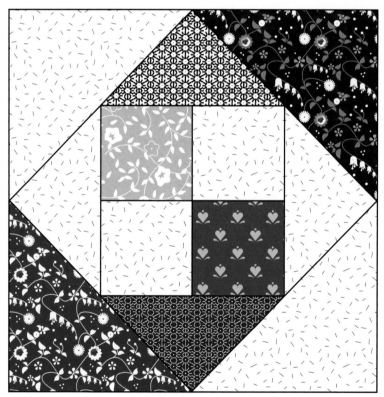

Illustration 3
Add more triangles to build up the block

Cut (2) strips 5" x 42" each of background fabric. Cut into (16) 5" squares and cut again diagonally once into (32) half-square triangles. You may use template #1 to cut these triangles.

Cut (3) strips 1⅜" x 42" each of the four reds and four grays. Sew each set of grouping strips together from dark to light. Press seams open. Using template #1, cut (32) variegated groupings (triangles) of each color set, placing base of template on darkest fabric. You will be adding these to complete the square, alternating with the background triangles as you did in the previous steps (Illus. 4). Note from the author: Exact increments cannot be achieved on your ruler, so measurements for each strip have been rounded up to 1⅜" for these strips.

Square off to 8½" blocks. You should have 16 completed blocks. Arrange in rows of four together, as shown in Illustration 5. Sew together and press.

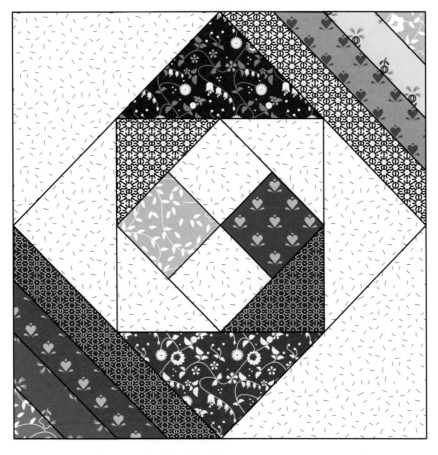

Illustration 4
Add your variegated segments to the block.

Illustration 5
Quilt block placement for MONKEYING AROUND

Borders:

For first border, cut (4) 1½" strips of background fabric. Sew to top and bottom of quilt top first, then add sides.

For second border, sew 1½" strips from each variegated fabric end to end to create second border strips. Sew to first border, top and bottom first, then add sides. (Refer to quilt photograph on page 45.)

Sew on binding to finish.

Estelle

ESTELLE, 36" x 36"
Designed by Linda Glantz
Quilted by Pat Young

Materials:

1 yd. background fabric

1 yd. dark green

¼ yd. dark gold

¼ yd. medium gold

¼ yd. light gold

¼ yd. dark green for first border

⅜ yd. light gold for second border

⅝ yd. for bias binding

1½ yds. for backing

Cut:

From background fabric –

(1) 2½" x 42" strip. Re-cut into (16) 2½" squares. Template #1 is provided in the pattern section for hand cutting.

(2) 8⅞" strips. Cut into (8) 8⅞" squares and then cut on the diagonal once into half-square triangles, or use template #2.

(1) 9" x 18" rectangle

(1) 9" x 15" rectangle

(1) 22" square for making bias 2¼" – 2½" strips for binding

From dark green, cut –

(1) 9" x 18" rectangle

(1) 9" x 15" rectangle

(2) 3" strips, re-cut into (16) 3" squares. Re-cut again on the diagonal into 32 half-square triangles or use template #3.

From dark gold, (4) 1½" strips

From medium gold, (4) 1½" strips

From light gold, (2) 2" strips

Borders:

From dark green first border, cut (4) 1" strips.

From light gold second border, cut (4) 3½" strips from the width of the fabric. (Leftover cuts from variegated groupings will be added to corners.)

Magic triangles:

Refer to Chapter 5, page 22 for complete instructions.

Take the 9" x 18" and 9" x 15" dark green and background fabric rectangles and place them right sides together. You will have two sets. Draw 3" square grid lines on wrong side of top fabric, then draw diagonal lines through each 3" square. Sew ¼" on either side of the diagonal lines (Illus. 1).

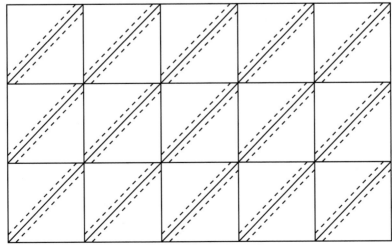

Illustration 1
Sewing triangles together into squares

Cut apart on grid lines, then diagonal lines, press to the dark side, and square up to 2½". You will need 60 magic triangles of dark green and background fabric sewn together. (For individual cutting, template #3 is also provided.)

Next sew the gold variegated strips together. You will need to sew two sets together in order to cut enough triangles. Using Template #4, Variegreat! cut (16) triangles from these strips (Illus. 2). You should get (12) cuts per strip, so you will have some left over.

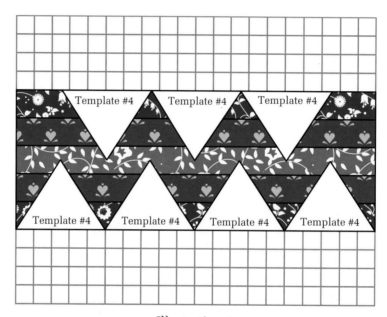

Illustration 2
Position templates to cut triangles from variegated
grouping segments.

Assembly line sew the remainder of the magic triangles together adding the 2½" background square to the bottom of 16 sets, as shown in Unit 1. Press toward the background square. Add a separate dark green triangle to this group (Unit 2). You will have 16 sets.

Sew this new strip to the other side of the variegated grouping (Unit 3) you already have cut and sewn together. Press toward the triangle.

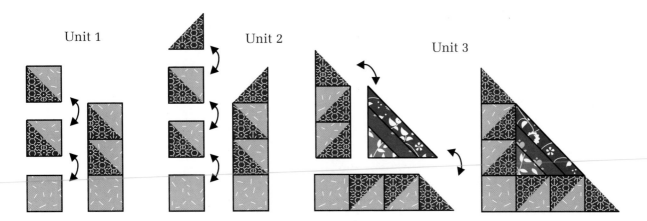

Illustration 3
Sewing units together

Sew this set to the large 8⅞" half-square triangle you cut from the background fabric. You should now have an 8½" square (Illus. 4).

Illustration 4
Variegated block design

Lay out blocks according to diagram (Illus. 5). Sew the vertical rows together and press. Join rows.

Illustration 5
Quilt block placement for ESTELLE

Sew on dark border strips to completed blocks. Press toward the border. For second border, using leftover pieces from variegated groupings, assemble 4 strips. Sew extra variegated pieces onto each end of the gold strips. Strip length must match the side of the quilt you will be adding the border to, so adjust center piece length to accommodate variegated pieces. Sew on border as one piece. (Refer to quilt photograph on page 51.)

Add binding as desired.

Follow the diagram below to assemble the Desert Star quilt (Illus. 5).

Illustration 5
Quilt block placement for DESERT STAR

For first border, sew dark border strips to opposite sides of the quilt. Assemble outer border. (Refer to quilt photograph on page 57.)

Quilt and bind as desired.

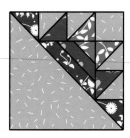

Diamond Lill

DIAMOND LILL, 45" x 45"
Designed by Linda Glantz
Quilted by Barb Rouse

Materials:

2⅛ yds. gray background fabric

1 yd. pink

1 yd. medium red

1 yd. burgundy

½ yd. burgundy for binding

Cut:

(6) 1½" strips each of pink, red, and burgundy

(5) 8½" x 42" strips from gray background fabric. Re-cut these strips again into 8½" squares. You can get four squares out of each 42" strip. Set four squares aside for corner blocks. Cut (16) squares into (32) half-square triangles or use template #1 on page 120.

Cut remaining fabric into (32) 2¾" gray squares for blocks or use template #2.

(2) 9" x 18" gray background fabric pieces

(2) 9" x 15" gray background fabric pieces

Also for background, cut:

(1) 9" x 18" pink fabric pieces

(1) 9" x 15" pink fabric pieces

(1) 9" x 18" medium-red fabric pieces

(1) 9" x 15" medium-red fabric pieces

(2) 2¾" strips burgundy into (32) 2¾" squares. Re-cut the squares into (64) half-square triangles or use template #3.

(5) 2½" strips of burgundy on cross grain for straight-edge binding

For variegation:

Sew 1½" strips of pink, red, and burgundy in groups of three together lengthwise, beginning with burgundy, then red, then pink (dark to light). Press seams open. Lay strip lengthwise on cutting mat with burgundy on the bottom and the pink on top. You should get six triangles from each strip. Use the Variegreat! template #4 to cut (32) triangles. Set aside.

Place one gray background 9" x 18" piece and one pink background 9" x 18" piece right sides together. Place another gray background 9" x 18" piece and one medium-red background 9" x 18" piece, right sides together. Draw a 3" grid on lighter fabric of each pair of fabrics. Refer to magic triangles instructions in Chapter 5, page 22, and follow the directions to mark, sew, and cut (32) half-square triangles needed in these two colors.

Do the same with the 9" x 15" pairs. Sew ¼" on each side of drawn lines on grid beginning in the lower left corner of the grid. After all lines are sewn, cut apart on the grid lines in between seams creating (30) half-square triangles sewn together. Press all triangles to the dark to create squares. Square off to 2¾".

Creating units:

Sew one pink/gray triangle unit to one red/gray triangle unit. Add one burgundy triangle. Press the seams in the same direction. Make 32 of these units (Illus. 1).

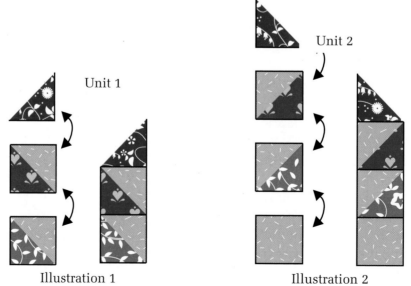

Unit 1

Unit 2

Illustration 1

Illustration 2

Creating units 1 and 2

Sew one gray 2¾" square to a pink/gray triangle unit; sew this to a red/gray triangle unit. Add one burgundy triangle. Press seams in one direction. Make 32 of these units (Illus. 2).

Sew one Unit 1 to the right side of your variegated grouping triangle. Then, sew one Unit 2 to the left side of your variegated grouping triangle. Repeat this process to make (32) Variegreat! units (Illus. 3). When the total triangle unit is together, check long side of unit and trim any excess fabric, leaving ¼" seam allowance.

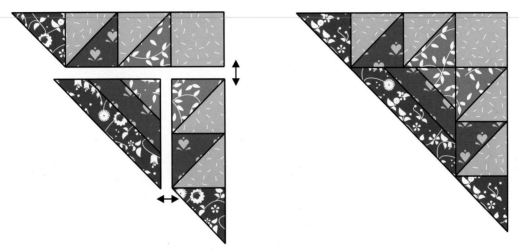

Illustration 3
Sew Unit 1 to right side of variegated triangle and Unit 2 to left side.

Sew these units to the 8½" half-square background triangles (template #1) to create a large square. Square off to measure 8½" (Illus. 4).

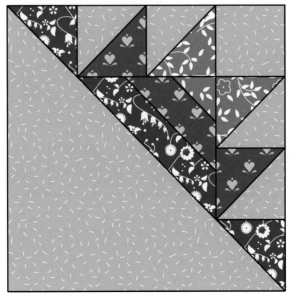

Illustration 4
DIAMOND LILL completed block

Sew squares together as shown in diagram. (Refer to quilt photograph on page 62.) Bind and quilt as desired.

Illustration 5
Quilt block placement for DIAMOND LILL

Illustration 5
Quilt block placement for CIRCLE OF FRIENDS

For first border, cut (4) 2½" x 42" strips from background fabric and sew one strip to the top of the quilt, one strip to the bottom of the quilt, and one strip each to both sides of the quilt.

For second border, cut (4) 1½" x 42" strips of medium blue and attach in same manner as first border. Cut (5) 1" x 42" strips of medium pink, purple, yellow, and green. Attach consecutively in a pleasing arrangement to blue border. (Refer to quilt photograph on page 67.)

Quilt as desired and bind.

Selma

SELMA, 56" x 56"
Designed by Linda Glantz
Quilted by Sue Bryant

Materials:

3 yds. background fabric

½ yd. light peach

½ yd. peach

⅜ yd. medium rust

½ yd. dark rust

1 yd. purple

¾ yd. for 2½" bias binding

3½ yds. backing

From background fabric:

Cut (4) 2½" x 42" strips

Cut (3) 4½" x 42" strips, re-cut into (20) 2½" x 4½" rectangles (template #1)

Cut (3) 4½" x 42" strips, re-cut into (24) 4½" squares (template #2)

Cut (1) 4⅞" x 42" strip, re-cut into (4) 4⅞" squares. Re-cut these once on the diagonal into 8 half-square triangles, or use template #4.

Cut (2) 12" squares. Re-cut these once on the diagonal into (4) half-square triangles for outside corners of the quilt.

Cut (11) 1½" x 42" strips for inside and outside borders

Cut (12) 2½" x 42" strips for Seminole border

From variegated fabrics:

Cut (4) 1½" x 42" strips of medium rust

Cut (8) 1½" x 42" strips of peach

Cut (8) 2" x 42" strips of light peach

From dark rust, cut:

Cut (2) 2⅞" x 42" strips and re-cut them into (28) 2⅞" squares. Cut on the diagonal to make 56 half-square triangles, or use template #4.

Cut (1) 6⅛" x 42" strip, re-cut into (5) 6⅛" squares or use template #5.

Cut (1) 3⅛" x 42" strip, re-cut into (4) 3⅛" x 6⅛" rectangles or use template #6.

From purple:

Cut (4) 2½" x 42" strips

Cut (2) 4½" x 42" strips. Re-cut them into (28) 2½" x 4½" rectangles for blocks or use template #1.

Cut (6) 2½" x 42" strips for Seminole border

For variegated grouping strips:

Sew strips together lengthwise (Illus. 1). You will need to make four long grouping strips. From these strips, cut (24) triangles, using Variegreat! triangle template #3. Reverse template #3

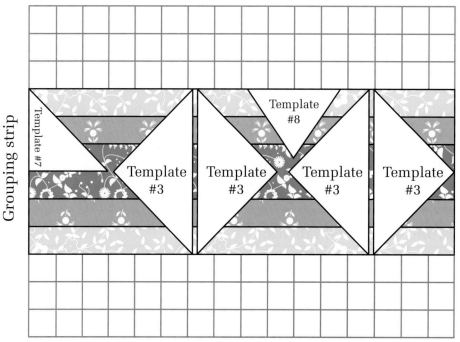

Illustration 1
Place templates on grouping strip and cut as needed.

when cutting to save fabric from your grouping strip (Illus. 1). Template #7 is a left and right cut.

Illustration 2

Sew (4) of these groupings to each 6⅛" dark rust square (Illus. 3). You will have 5 Variegreat! blocks.

Illustration 3
Sew grouping triangles to each side of 6⅛" square.

From the rest of the grouping strips, cut (4) left and (4) right of template #7. Sew these to the left and right sides of the (4) 3⅛" x 6⅛" dark rust rectangles to make Unit 3 of the four half-blocks for centering on quilt sides (Illus. 4).

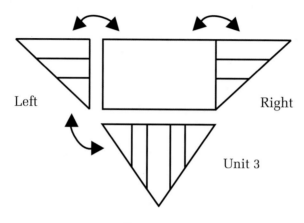

Left   Right

Unit 3

Illustration 4
Making Unit 3, center for half-blocks
for centers of quilt sides.

From the leftover variegated strips in Illus. 1, cut (28) template #8 triangles from the medium and light portion of the strip. The full-size pattern pieces for the variegated pieces are also provided on page 124 – 126 for your convenience in cutting and sewing by hand.

To the left and right sides of these variegated triangles, sew the dark rust 2⅞" half-square triangles (Illus. 5).

Rust   **Rust**

Illustration 5
Sew half-square triangles to each side of the variegated triangle.

Attach purple 2½" x 4½" rectangles to the bottom of that grouping.

Next, sew 2½" strips of purple and background fabric together lengthwise. Press seam toward dark fabric. Sew and press four of these. Re-cut strips on the width every 2½". You will need 56 sets of these background and purple rectangles. Attach one set to each side of previous grouping (Illus. 6). You will have 28 of these groupings.

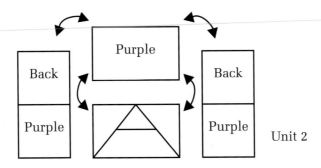

Illustration 6
Use eight of these with Unit 3 and a half-square triangle
to form (4) half-blocks for center of sides of quilt.

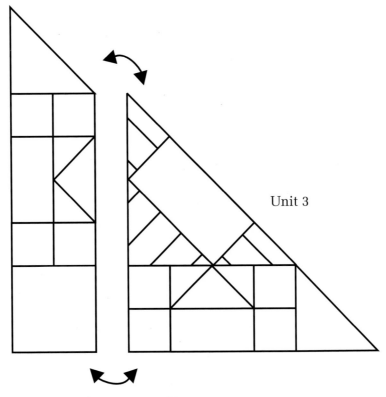

Illustration 7
Half block diagram

Sew (2) 4½" background squares to each end of 10 of these groupings. Leave the other 10 without the end squares; sew these to top and bottom of each of the 5 Variegreat! blocks. Then add the 10 sections with the end squares to the two opposite sides of the blocks (Illus. 8).

Illustration 8
Diagram of assembled quilt block.
Set on point for the finished quilt.

Assemble completed blocks and half-blocks with outside corner background triangles, following placement diagram (Illus. 9).

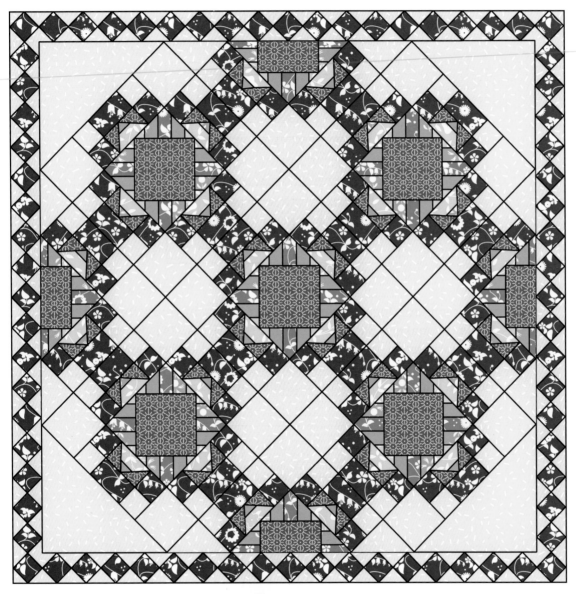

Illustration 9
Quilt block placement for SELMA with Seminole border (inner border not shown)

Instructions for Seminole border:

Attach first 1½" background border strips to all sides of quilt for inside border.

With the 2½" strips of background fabric and purple, sew strips together lengthwise in the following order: background, purple, background. Press seams in one direction. Cut strip set into 2½" segments (Illus. 10).

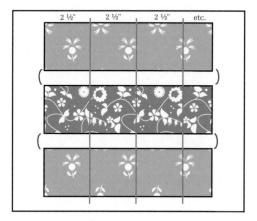

Illustration 10

Sew segments together, offset, with seams in opposite directions, to make a Seminole strip. Press (Illus. 11). Straighten ends for correct placement. Trim feathered edges. Sew Seminole strip to first border already attached to quilt. Then add 1½" outside border. (Refer to quilt photograph, page 72.)

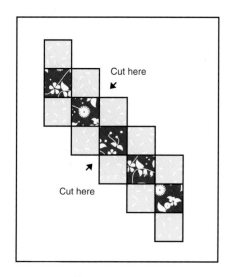

Illustration 11

Materials:

1¼ yds. light blue for background and points

⅝ yd. medium blue for diamonds and border

⅜ yd. bright color for corner triangles and squares

¼ yd. each of 6 blue color gradations

For darkest gradation, add ¼ yd. for borders

1¼ yds. backing fabric

¼ yd. binding

Cut:

(6) 1¾" strips of lightest variegation color

(6) 1⅜" strips each of the other 5 gradation fabrics

Sew strips together from light to dark. You will have six sets of strips. Using Template #1, Variegreat! cut (36) variegated triangles from these strips, placing the template so that the base of the triangle is on the darkest fabric.

For light background triangles; using template #2, cut (96) triangles. Use (72) pieces for the blocks and (24) pieces in the borders.

From medium blue, cut (12) triangles for border using template #2 and cut (36) diamonds using template #3.

(18) 3⅞" squares from bright fabric (or beast fabric) for block corners. Quick-cut half-square triangles for a total of (36) pieces or use template #4. Full-size templates are provided for hand cutting in the pattern section.

To assemble squares, sew two light triangles to either side of one blue diamond. Make (36) of these units (Illus. 1).

Illustration 1
Sew triangles to either side of diamond.

Then, sew bright fabric half-square triangle to base of variegated triangles. Again, you will have (36) units. Next, sew diamond unit to right side of variegated unit (Illus. 2). Assemble four of these combined units to complete the block. The nine finished blocks should each measure 12½".

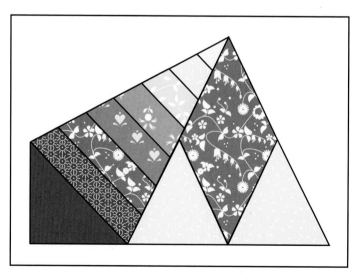

Illustration 2
Sew diamond unit to side of variegated unit.

For border:

Cut a total of (24) pieces, cut (12) pieces from the dark border fabric using template #5, then reverse the template and cut (12) more.

Quick-cut (4) 3⅜" corner squares of bright colored fabric or use template #6.

Using the light triangles and medium color triangles, sew light together as shown below (Illus. 3). Adjust for seam allowance.

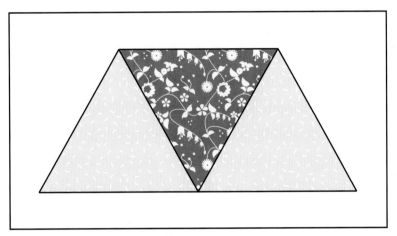

Illustration 3
Sew two light triangles to both sides of a dark triangle.

Add dark border pieces to triangle units and then corners to each end of two units (Illus. 4). Sew borders to the quilt. Quilt and bind as desired. (Refer to quilt photograph, page 88.)

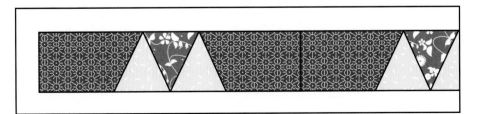

Illustration 4
Border piece placement

Illustration 5
Quilt block placement for BEAUTY & THE BEAST

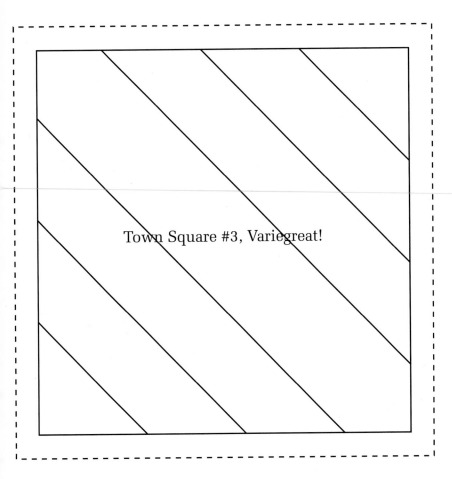

Town Square #3, Variegreat!

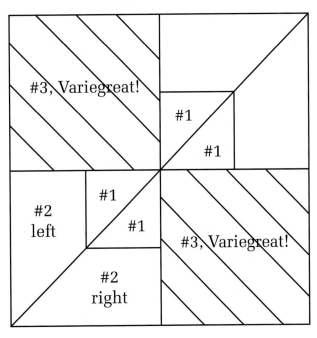

#3, Variegreat!

#1

#1

#2
left

#1

#1

#2
right

#3, Variegreat!

Template placement diagram for TOWN SQUARE

Mint Julep Templates

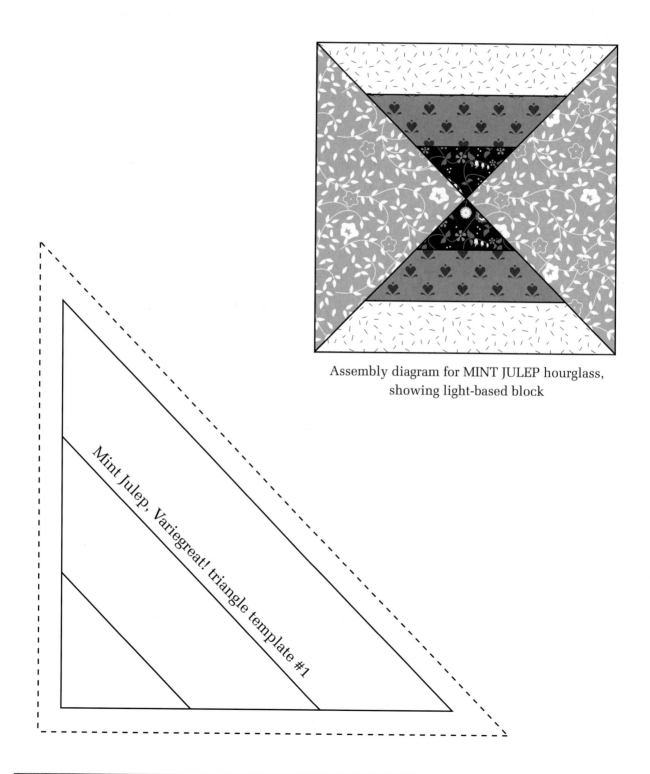

Assembly diagram for MINT JULEP hourglass,
showing light-based block

Mint Julep, Variegreat! triangle template #1

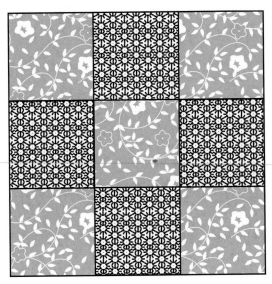

Assembly diagram for MINT JULEP Nine-Patch

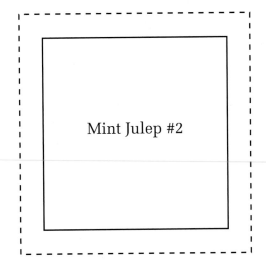

Mint Julep #2

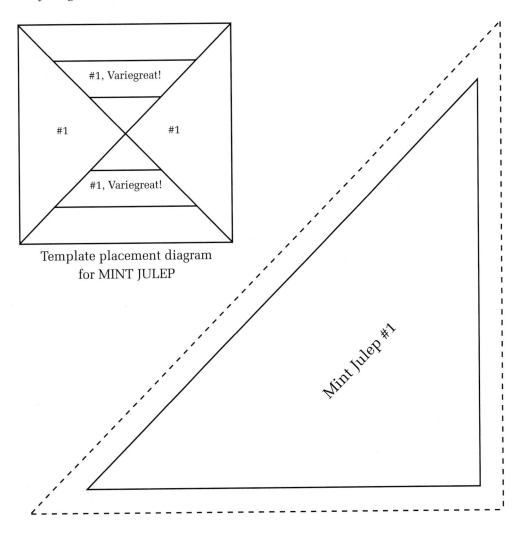

#1, Variegreat!

#1   #1

#1, Variegreat!

Template placement diagram
for MINT JULEP

Mint Julep #1

Assembly diagram for RUTHIE

Ruthie Templates

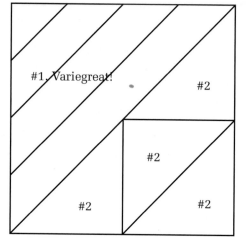

Template placement diagram for RUTHIE

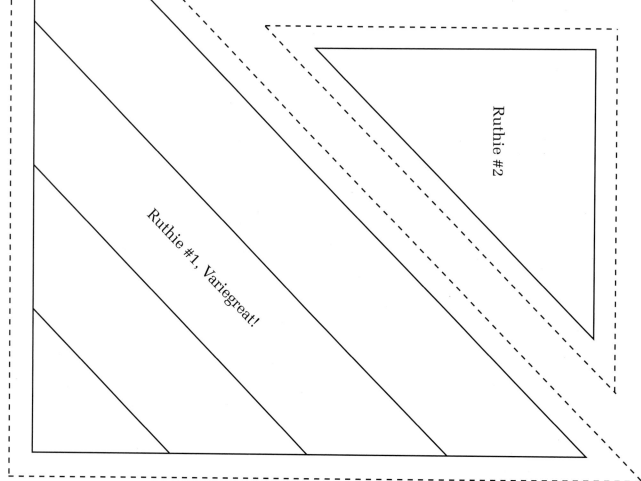

Ruthie #1, Variegreat!

Ruthie #2

In The Pines Templates

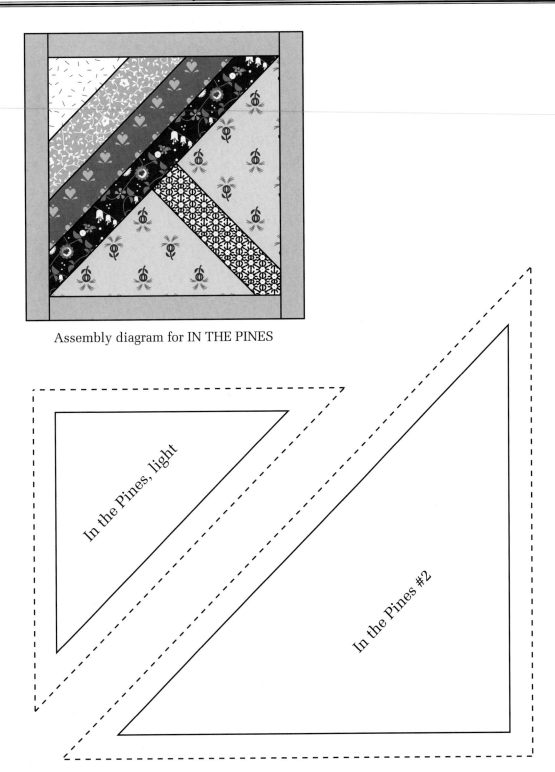

Assembly diagram for IN THE PINES

In the Pines, light

In the Pines #2

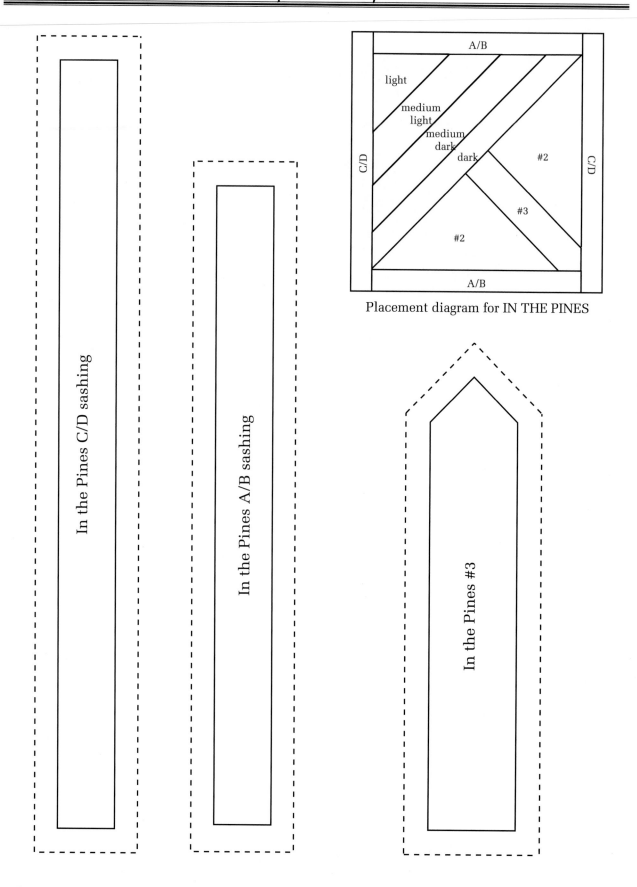

Placement diagram for IN THE PINES

In the Pines C/D sashing

In the Pines A/B sashing

In the Pines #3

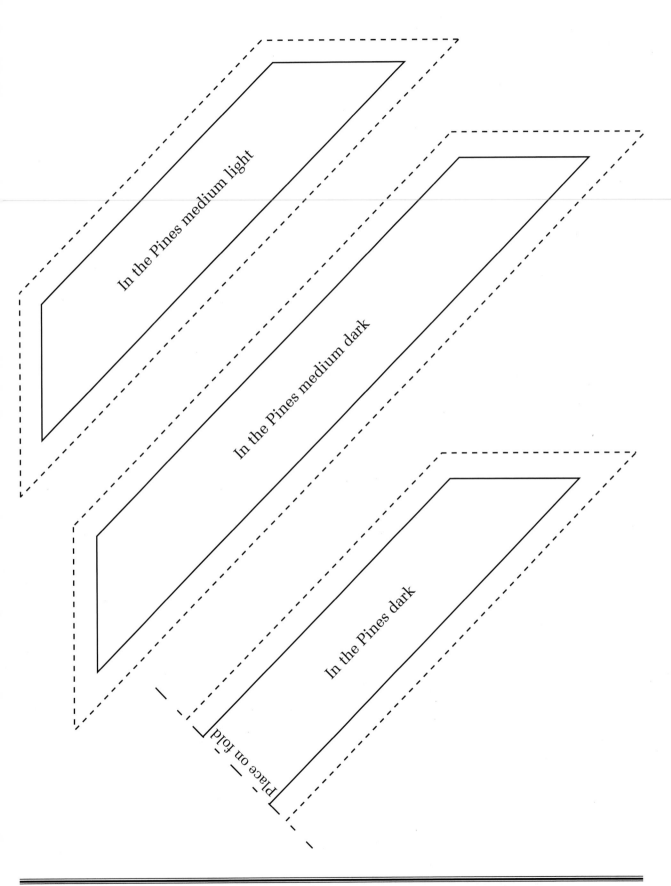

In the Pines medium light

In the Pines medium dark

In the Pines dark

place on fold

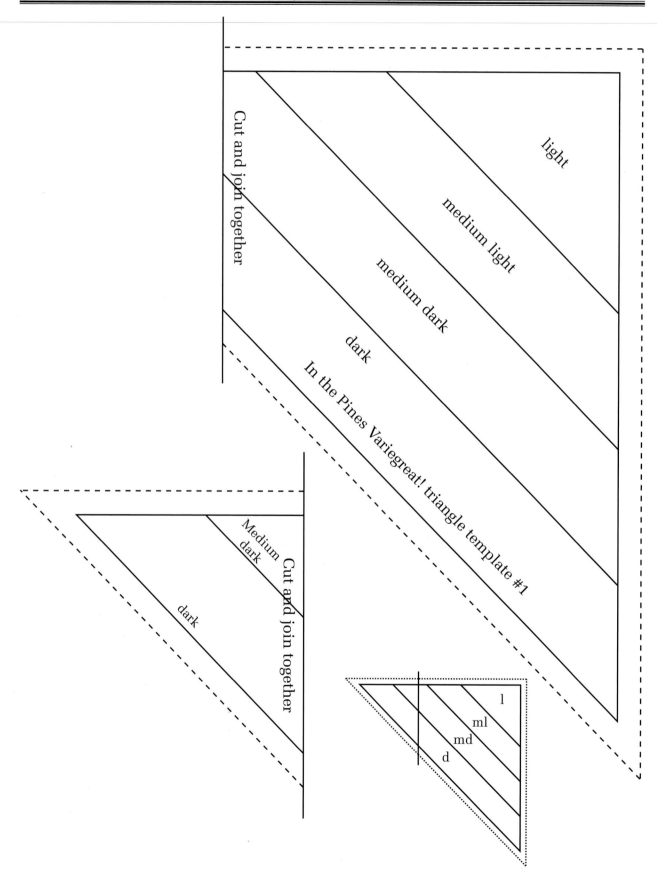

light

medium light

medium dark

dark

Cut and join together

In the Pines Variegreat! triangle template #1

Medium dark

dark

Cut and join together

l

ml

md

d

Monkeying Around Templates

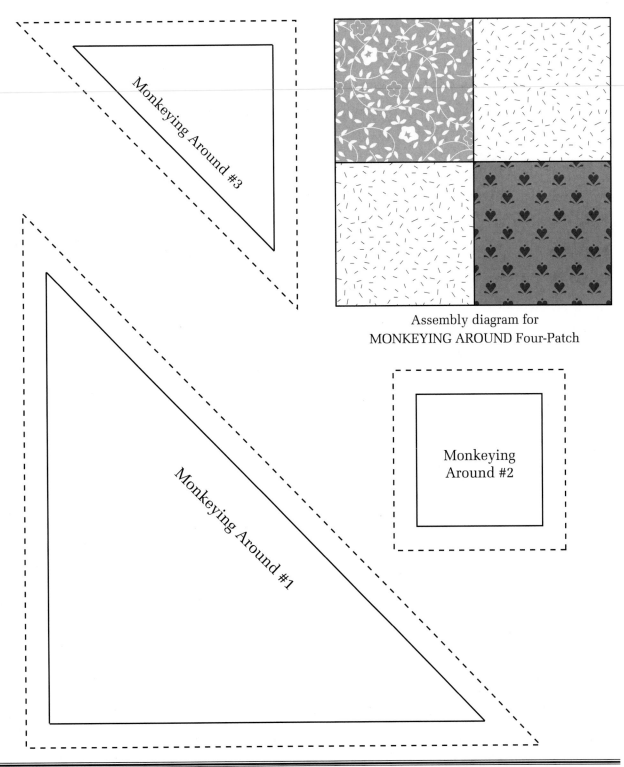

Monkeying Around #3

Monkeying Around #1

Monkeying Around #2

Assembly diagram for
MONKEYING AROUND Four-Patch

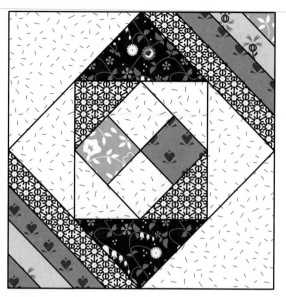

Assembly diagram for MONKEYING AROUND

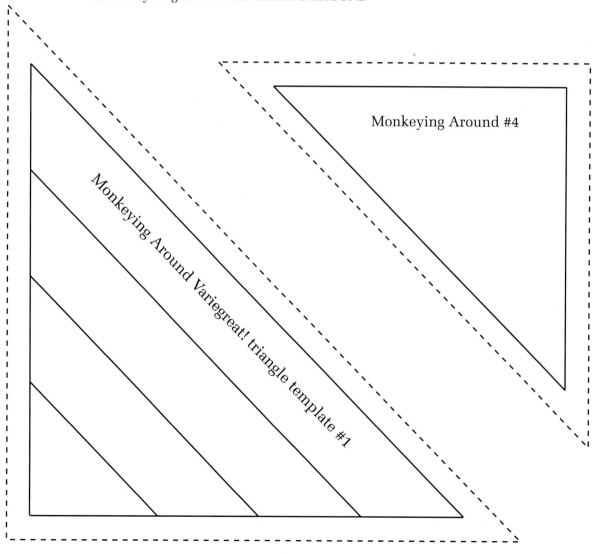

Monkeying Around #4

Monkeying Around Variegreat! triangle template #1

Estelle Templates

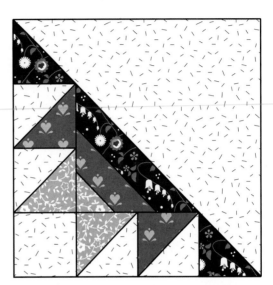

Assembly diagram for ESTELLE

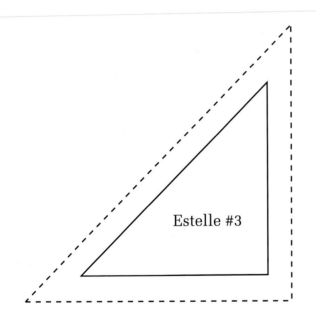

Estelle #3

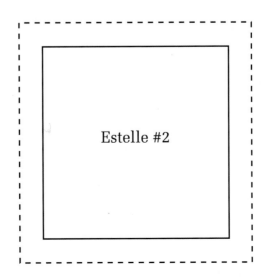

Estelle #2

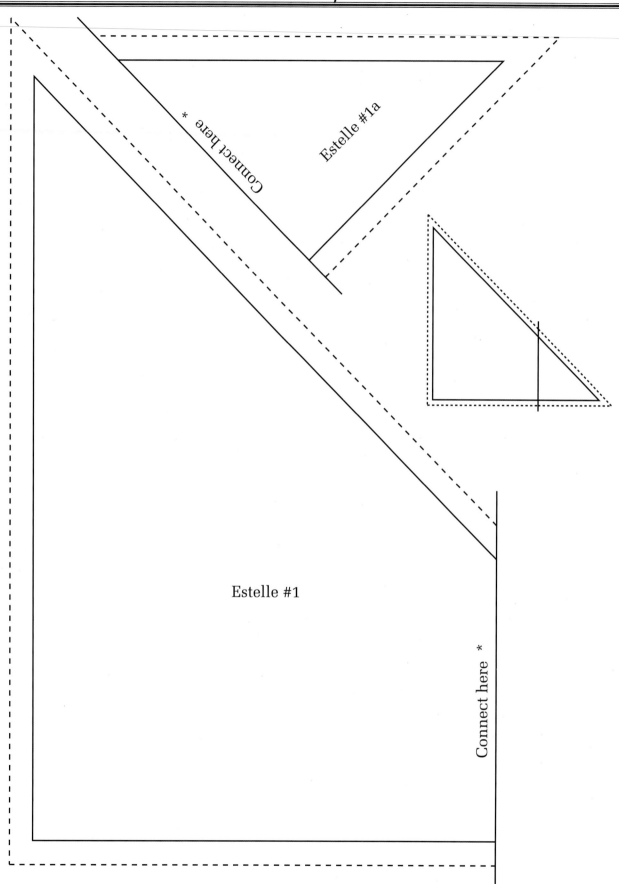

Estelle #1a

Connect here *

Estelle #1

Connect here *

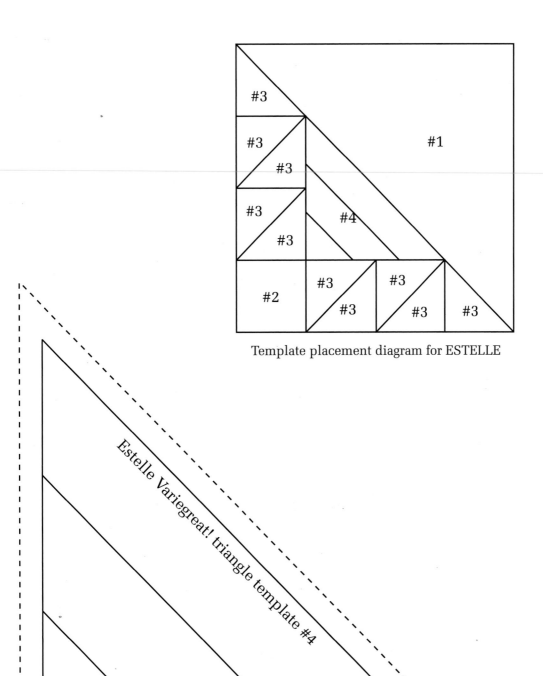

Template placement diagram for ESTELLE

Estelle half of 8½" square
for corner blocks

Place on fold to make 8½" square

Assembly diagram for DESERT STAR

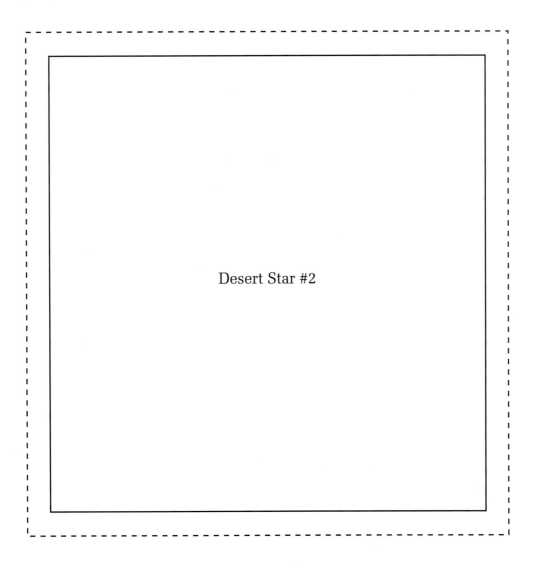

Desert Star #2

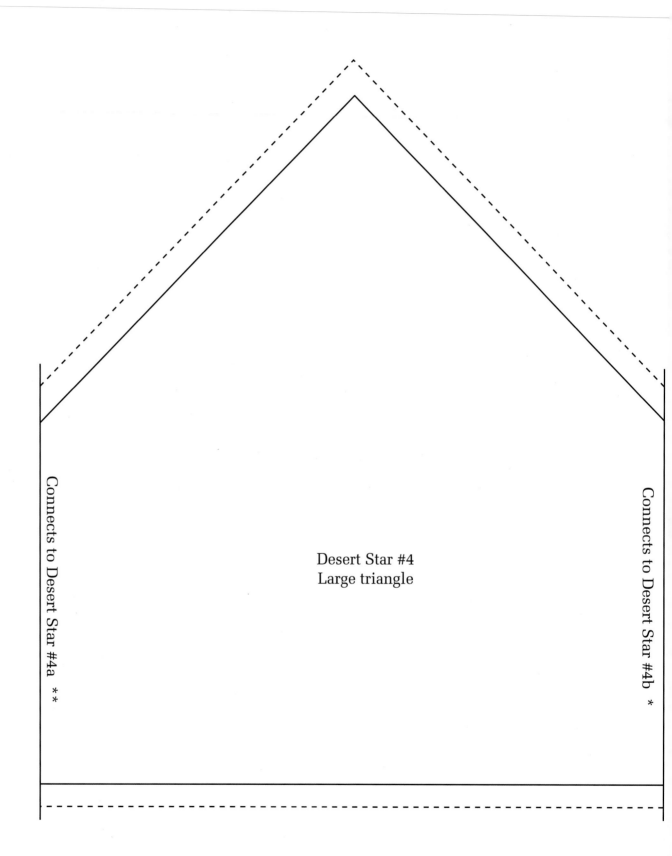

Desert Star #4
Large triangle

Connects to Desert Star #4a **

Connects to Desert Star #4b *

Diamond Lill Templates

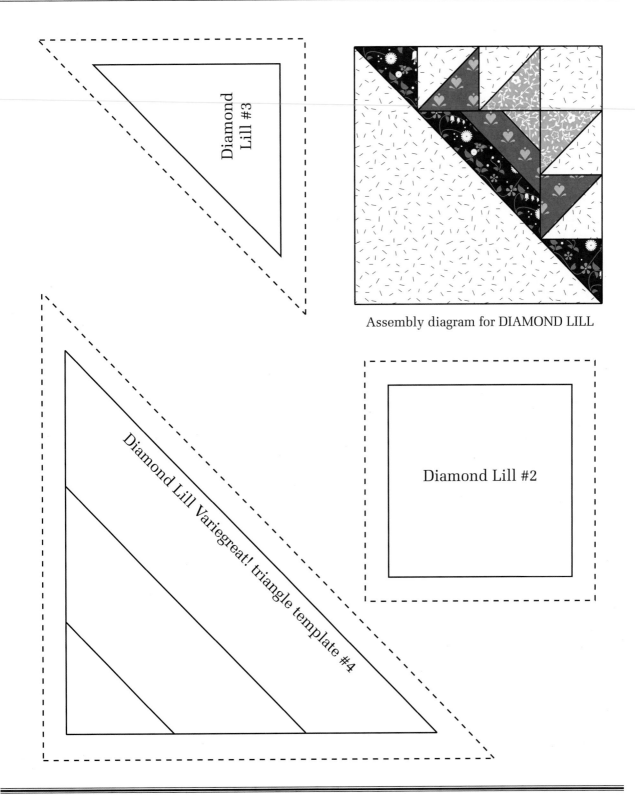

Diamond
Lill #3

Assembly diagram for DIAMOND LILL

Diamond Lill Variegreat! triangle template #4

Diamond Lill #2

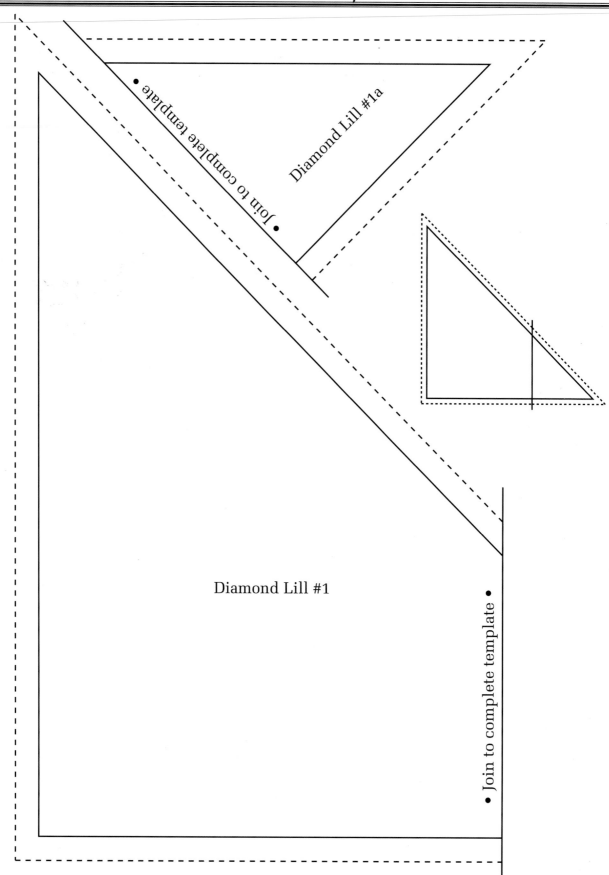

Diamond Lill #1a

Join to complete template

Diamond Lill #1

Join to complete template

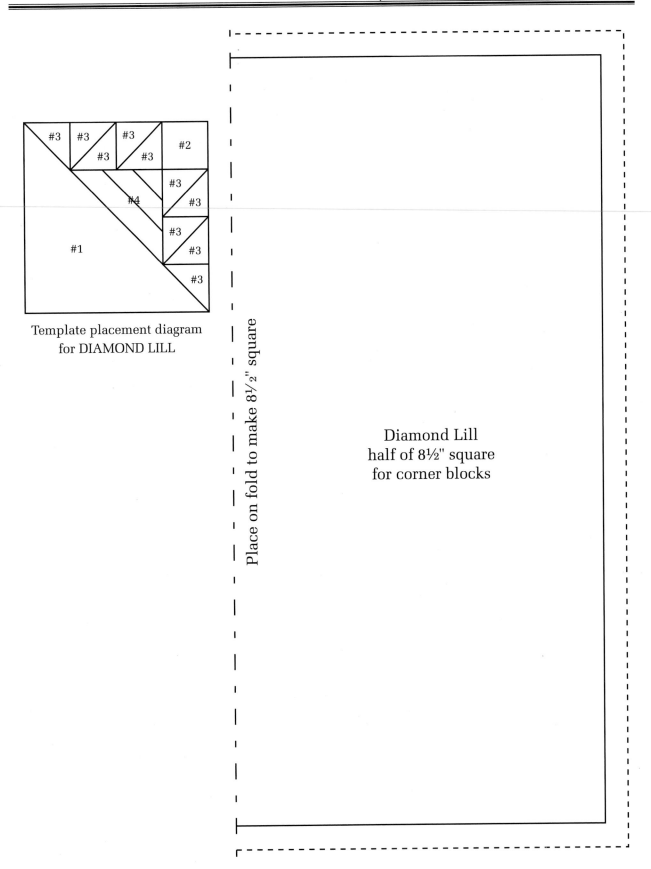

Template placement diagram
for DIAMOND LILL

#3 #3 #3 #2
#3 #3
#3
#4 #3
#3
#1 #3
#3

Place on fold to make 8½" square

Diamond Lill
half of 8½" square
for corner blocks

Circle of Friends Templates

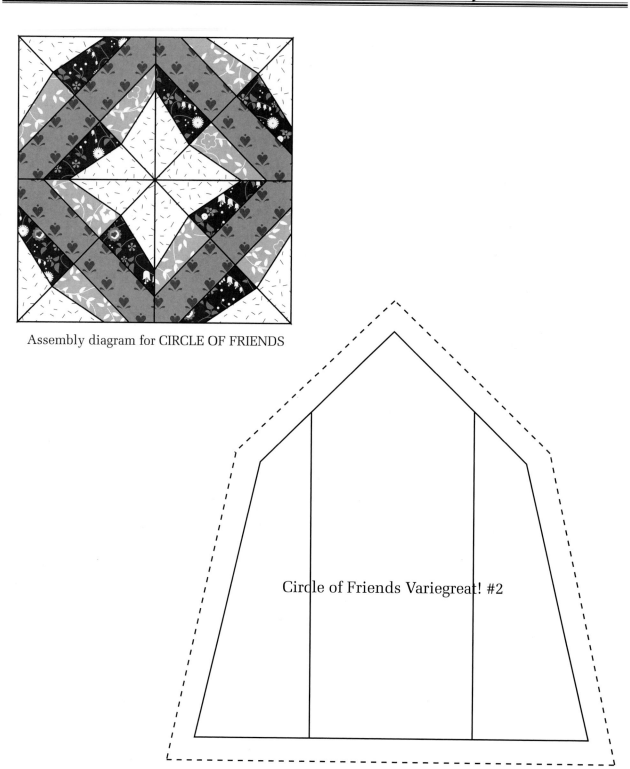

Assembly diagram for CIRCLE OF FRIENDS

Circle of Friends Variegreat! #2

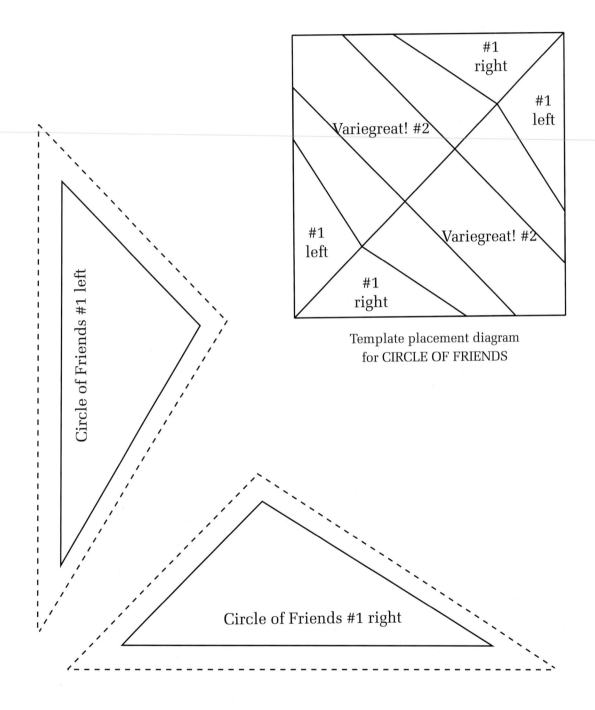

Template placement diagram
for CIRCLE OF FRIENDS

Circle of Friends #1 left

Circle of Friends #1 right

Assembly diagram for SELMA

Selma Templates

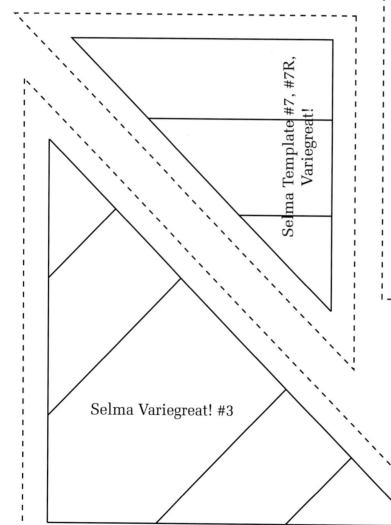

Selma #1

Selma Template #7, #7R,
Variegreat!

Selma Variegreat! #3

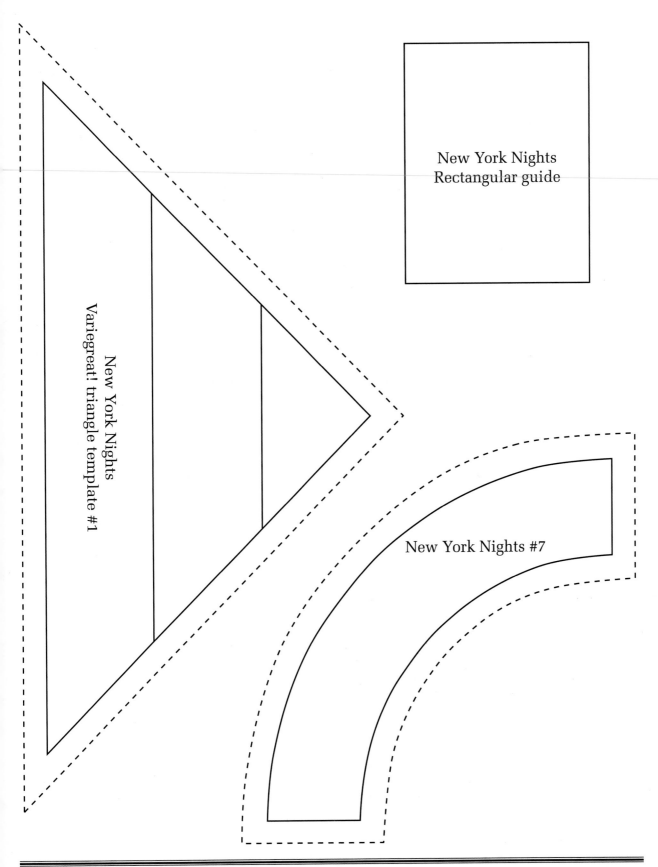

New York Nights
Rectangular guide

New York Nights
Variegreat! triangle template #1

New York Nights #7

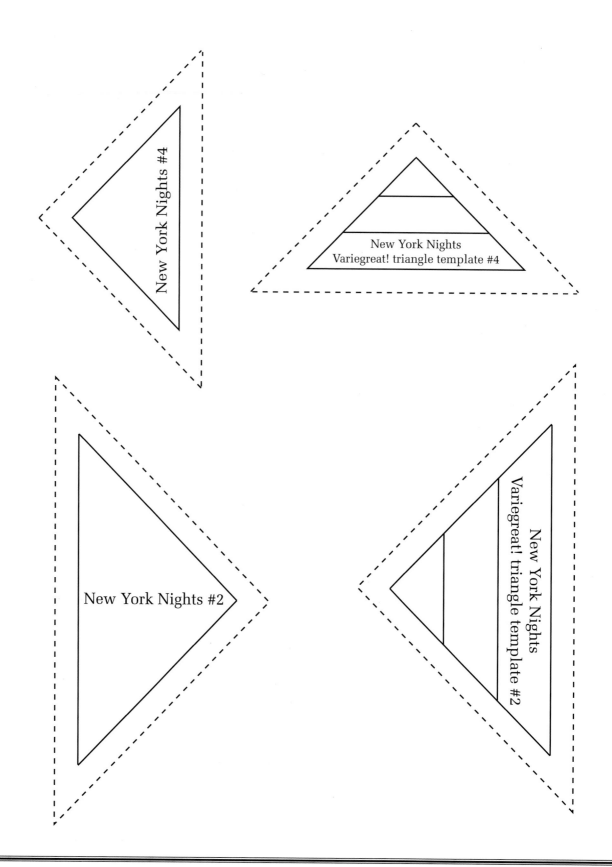

New York Nights #4

New York Nights
Variegreat! triangle template #4

New York Nights #2

New York Nights
Variegreat! triangle template #2

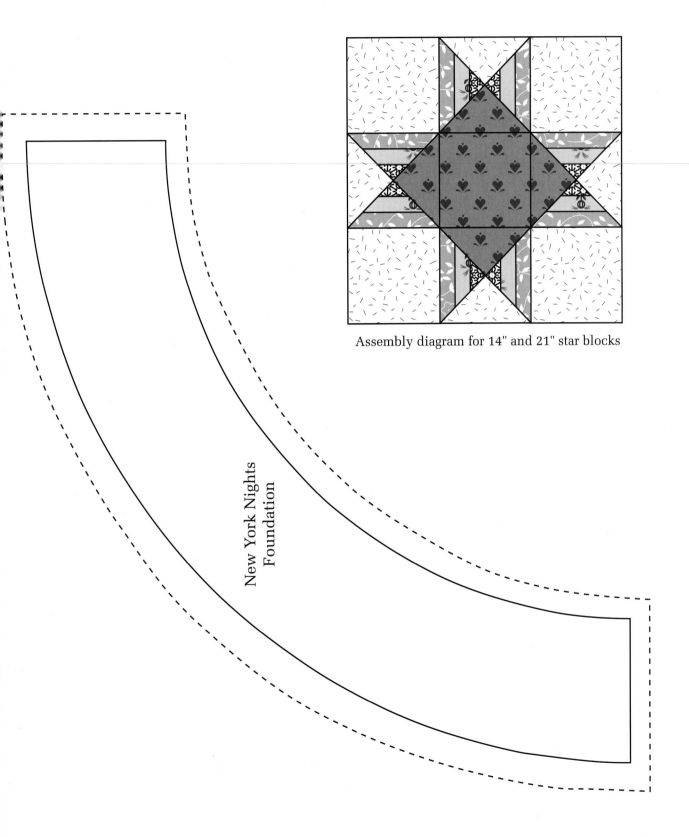

Assembly diagram for 14" and 21" star blocks

New York Nights
Foundation

*Without seams

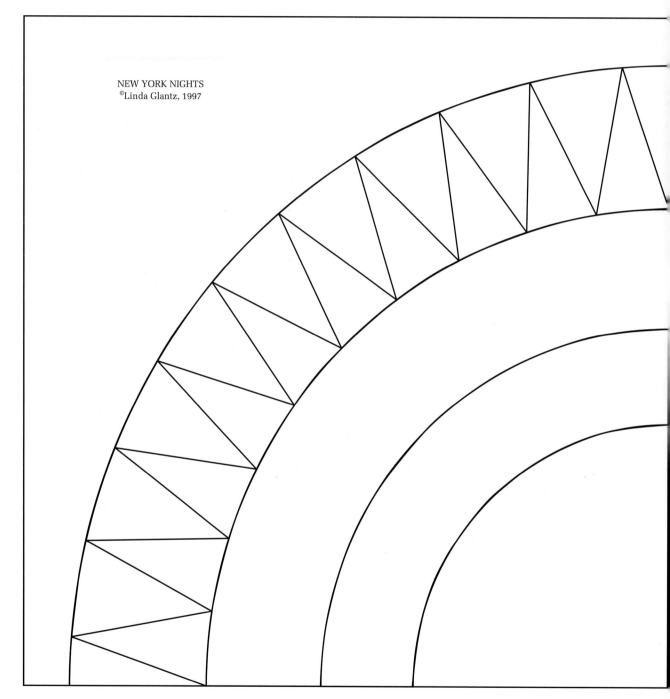

NEW YORK NIGHTS
©Linda Glantz, 1997

New York Beauty – Paper-piecing foundation.

The author and publisher give permission to photocopy this pattern. Slight distortions will occur.

*Without seams

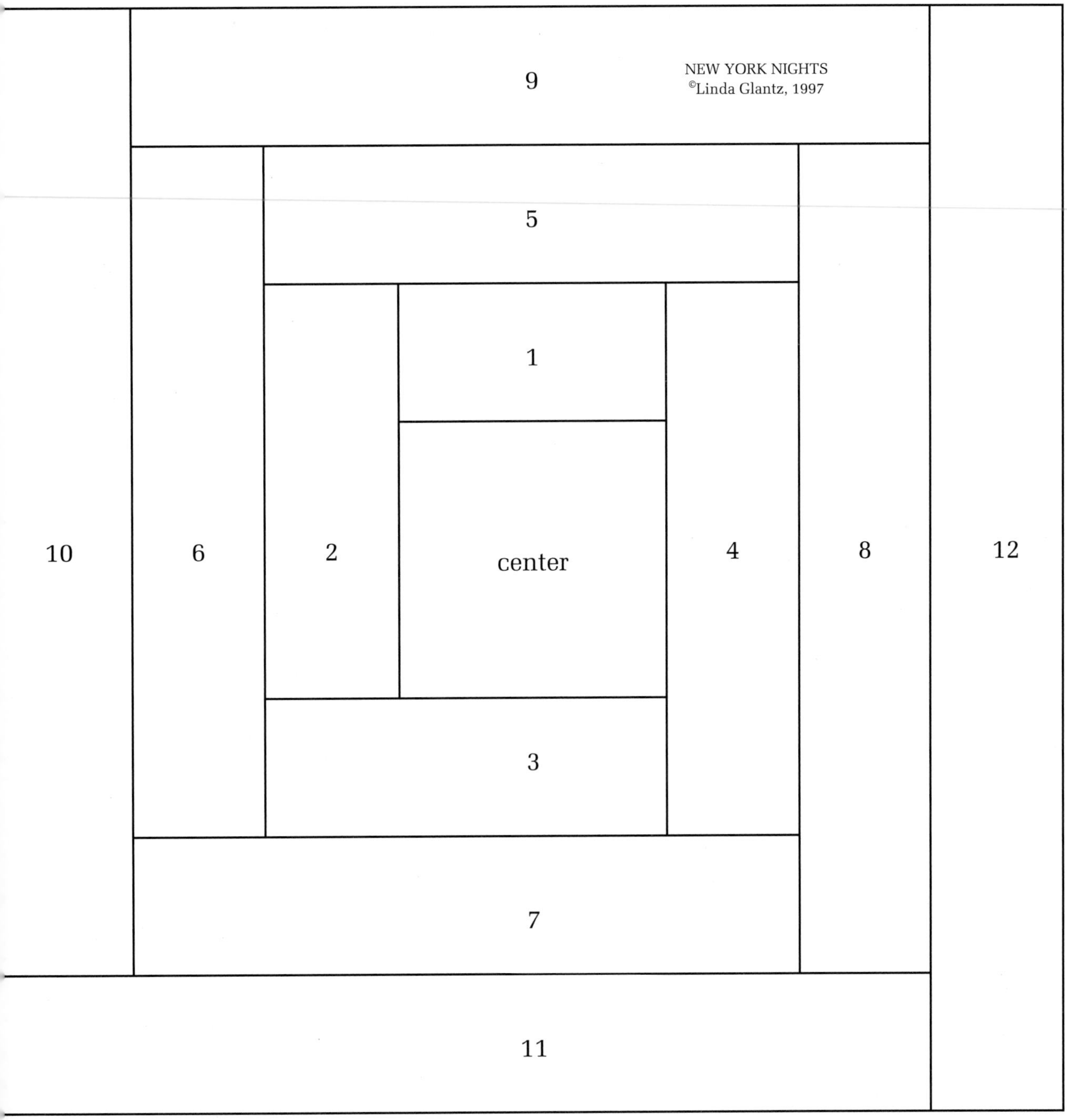

NEW YORK NIGHTS
©Linda Glantz, 1997

9

5

1

center

2

3

4

6

8

10

12

7

11

Log Cabin – Paper-piecing foundation.

The author and publisher give permission to photocopy this pattern. Slight distortions will occur.

New York Nights #5
7" Star

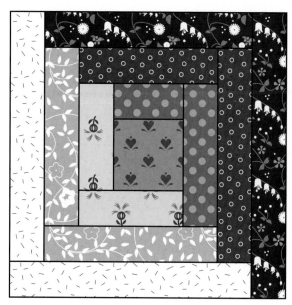

Assembly diagram for Log Cabin block

New York Nights #3
14" Star

Beauty & the Beast Templates

Assembly diagram for
BEAUTY & THE BEAST

Beauty & the Beast

Beauty & the Beast
Variegreat! triangle template #1

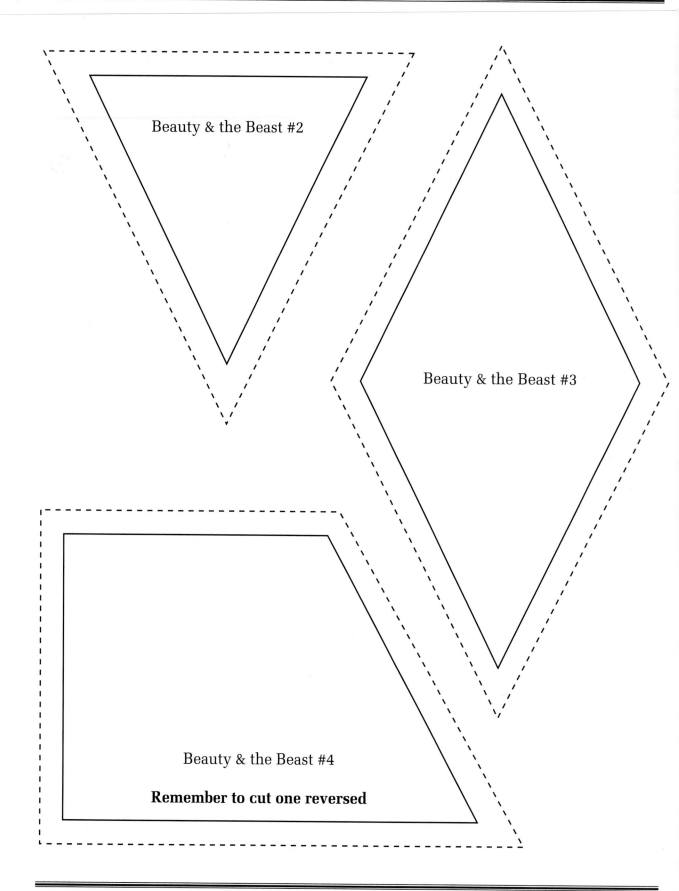

Beauty & the Beast #2

Beauty & the Beast #3

Beauty & the Beast #4

Remember to cut one reversed

Floral Fantasy Templates

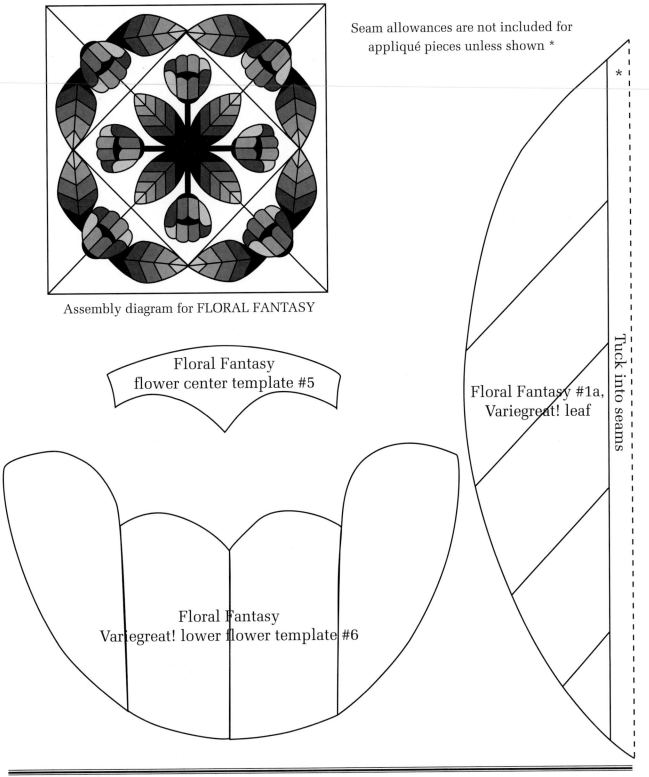

Assembly diagram for FLORAL FANTASY

Seam allowances are not included for appliqué pieces unless shown *

Floral Fantasy
flower center template #5

Floral Fantasy #1a,
Variegreat! leaf

Tuck into seams

Floral Fantasy
Variegreat! lower flower template #6

Place on fold to make 8½" square

Floral Fantasy #

Floral Fantasy
Variegreat! upper flower template #4

Seam allowances are not included
for appliqué pieces unless shown *

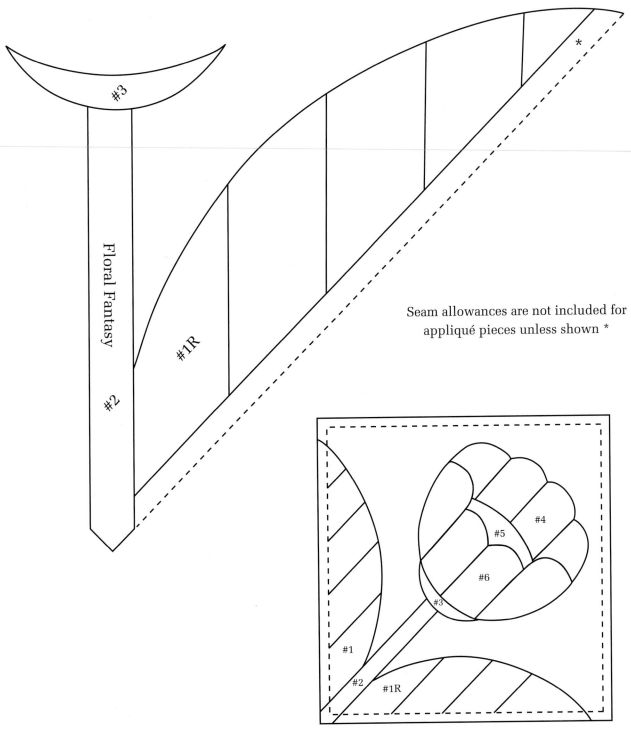

#3

Floral Fantasy

#1R

#2

*

Seam allowances are not included for appliqué pieces unless shown *

#4

#5

#6

#3

#1

#2 #1R

Template placement diagram for FLORAL FANTASY

Assembly and placement diagrams
for leaves in FLORAL FANTASY

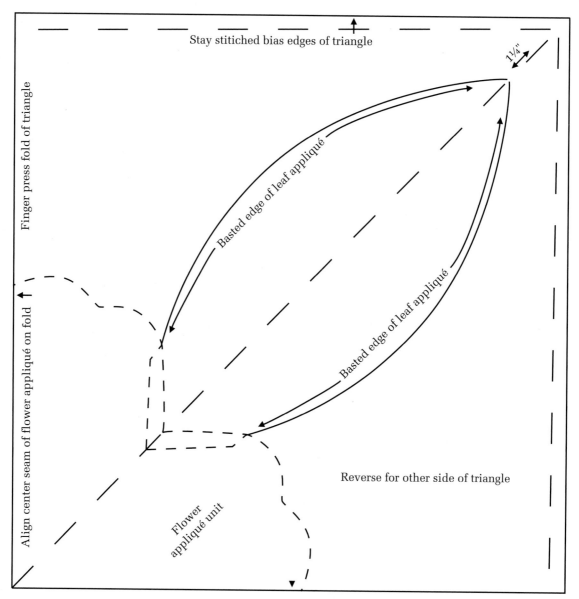

Stay stitched bias edges of triangle

Finger press fold of triangle

1¼"

Basted edge of leaf appliqué

Basted edge of leaf appliqué

Align center seam of flower appliqué on fold

Reverse for other side of triangle

Flower
appliqué unit

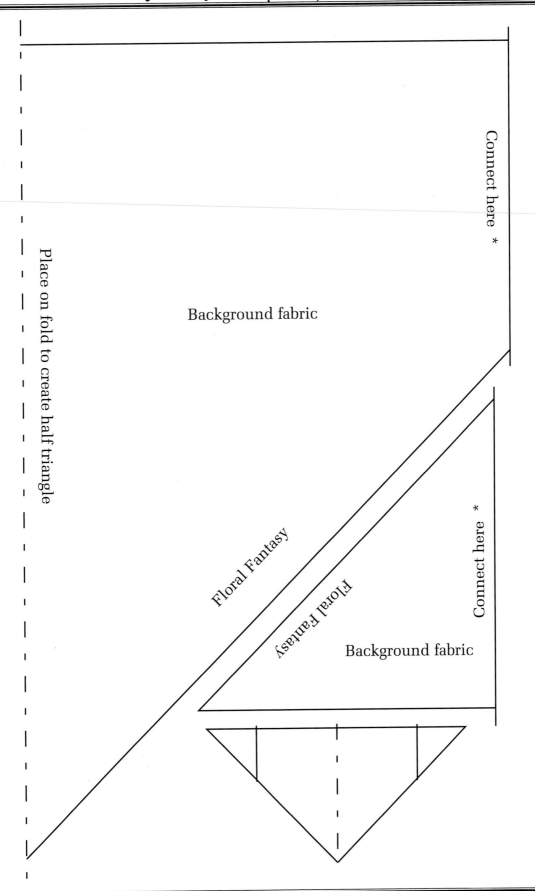

Connect here *

Place on fold to create half triangle

Background fabric

Floral Fantasy

Floral Fantasy

Connect here *

Background fabric

Bibliography

"Shortcuts," by Donna Lynn Thompson, That Patchwork Place

"Pioneer Sampler," by Eleanor Burns, Quilt In A Day

Electric Quilt 2, Quilt Design Computer Program

Country Neighbors Quilt Guild, Holley, New York

AQS Books on Quilts

This is only a partial listing of the books on quilts that are available from the American Quilter's Society. AQS books are known the world over for timely topics, clear writing, beautiful color photographs, and accurate illustrations and patterns. The following books are available from your local bookseller, quilt shop, or public library. If you are unable to locate certain titles in your area, you may order by mail from the AMERICAN QUILTER'S SOCIETY, P.O. Box 3290, Paducah, KY 42002-3290. Add $2.00 for postage for the first book ordered and 40¢ for each additional book. Include item number, title, and price when ordering. Allow 14 to 21 days for delivery. Customers with Visa, MasterCard, or Discover may phone in orders from 7:00–5:00 CST, Monday–Friday, Toll Free 1-800-626-5420.